The Bahamas

The Bahamas

By Martin Hintz

Enchantment of the World™
Second Series

Children's Press®

An Imprint of Scholastic Inc.

New York   Toronto   London   Auckland   Sydney
Mexico City   New Delhi   Hong Kong
Danbury, Connecticut

Frontispiece: Coconut palm in the Bahamas

Consultant: Keith F. Otterbein, PhD, Professor Emeritus, University at Buffalo, New York; Charlotte Swanson Otterbein, PhD

Special thanks to TheBahamasWeekly.com for their help with images.

Please note: All statistics are as up-to-date as possible at the time of publication.

Book production by The Design Lab

Library of Congress Cataloging-in-Publication Data
Hintz, Martin.
  The Bahamas/by Martin Hintz.
      p. cm.—(Enchantment of the world. Second series)
  Includes bibliographical references and index.
  ISBN: 978-0-531-27541-2 (lib. bdg.)
  1. Bahamas—Juvenile literature. I. Title.
  F1651.2.H66 2012
  972.96—dc23   2012000513

1 2 3 4 5 6 7 8 9 10 R 22 21 20 19 18 17 16 15 14 13

Acknowledgments

The author wishes to thank all the tourism, business, creative, and political personnel in the Bahamas who contributed their insights, knowledge, and vision about their country. Individual Bahamians went out of their way to help, always with a smile and a "no problem, man," even with the most difficult question or request. Everyone's enthusiastic support made this job easier. Special thanks to my wife, Pam, who is always a willing and able travel partner.

Contents

Cover photo:
Fishing in Abaco

CHAPTER

 ONE Good Day, Bahamas 8

TWO Water, Water Everywhere 14

THREE Glorious Life... 30

FOUR The Old Days...................................... 42

FIVE Running the Government.......................... 60

SIX Making Money 68

SEVEN A Mix of People................................. 80

EIGHT Spiritual Life....................................... 90

NINE Island Art.. 98

TEN Daily Doings 116

Eleuthera Island

Timeline **128**

Fast Facts **130**

To Find Out More **134**

Index **136**

Hawksbill turtle

Good Day, Bahamas

8

It's Junkanoo time! Here come the bands, dozens of people dressed in fancy headdresses and flowing skirts made of colorful streams of crepe paper. The more swirls and twirls, the better the show. The loud music of the Valley Boys, the Saxons, and other bands travels along Bay Street in downtown Nassau. The musicians pound goatskin drums and clatter cowbells. Shrill whistles and the sounds of brass horns fill the air. Everyone claps and sways to the beat. People peer down from balconies and shout greetings to their friends on the sidewalks below.

Junkanoo is a festival in the Bahamas that takes place in the early hours of December 26 and again early on New Year's Day. The celebration begins to heat up around 2:00 a.m. and lasts until at least 8:00 a.m. Junkanoo originated in the seventeenth century when enslaved workers were given a few days off around Christmas. They were allowed to leave their

Opposite: **A man dances in the Junkanoo festival in Nassau.**

plantations briefly and celebrate the holiday. They expressed their joy through music, dancing, and wearing costumes.

The origin of the term *junkanoo* is lost in the shadows of history. It might have evolved from "John Canoe," the name some Africans called the ship captains who hauled them in chains to the Americas. Others say it was the name of a heroic West African prince who stood up to the English in the Bahamas. Or perhaps it came from the French words

Junkanoo parades feature elaborate costumes and floats.

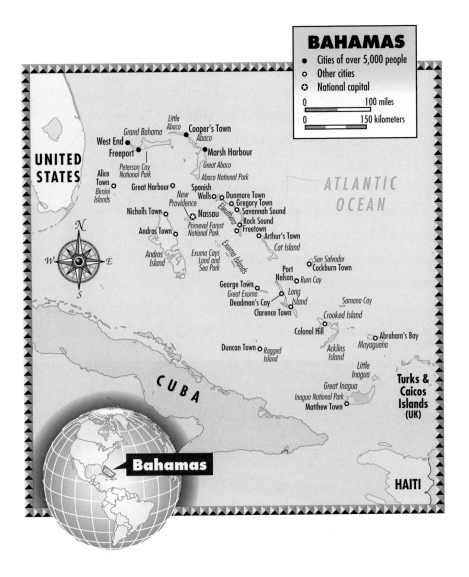

UNITED STATES

ATLANTIC OCEAN

Little Abaco

Cooper's Town

Grand Bahama

Abaco

West End

Freeport

Marsh Harbour

Great Abaco

Peterson Cay National Park

Abaco National Park

Alice Town

Great Harbour

Spanish Wells

Dunmore Town

Bimini Islands

New Providence

Gregory Town

Savannah Sound

Nicholls Town

Nassau

Rock Sound

Freetown

Andros Town

Primeval Forest National Park

Arthur's Town

Cat Island

Andros Island

Exuma Cays Land and Sea Park

San Salvador

Cockburn Town

Exuma Islands

Port Nelson

Rum Cay

George Town

Great Exuma

Long Island

Samana Cay

Deadman's Cay

Clarence Town

Crooked Island

Colonel Hill

Abraham's Bay

Mayaguana

Duncan Town

Ragged Island

Acklins Island

Little Inagua

CUBA

Turks & Caicos Islands (UK)

Great Inagua

Inagua National Park

Matthew Town

Bahamas

HAITI

gens inconnus, which mean "masked or unknown people." If a drummer is wearing a mask, no one knows if he is a politician or a fisher. Everyone joins in the wild celebration.

The largest Junkanoo celebration is in Nassau, the capital of the Bahamas. Nassau is a bustling place, filled with honking cars and crowded sidewalks.

Everywhere else in the nation is quieter. The country is made up of seven hundred islands, dots of land sprinkled across 100,000 square miles (260,000 square kilometers) of ocean to the southeast of the U.S. state of Florida. On many islands in the Bahamas, people enjoy glistening white sand beaches, quiet cafés serving freshly caught fish, warm breezes, and clear blue seas.

Bahamians often travel between Nassau, on the island of New Providence, and other parts of the country. These other islands are called the Family Islands or Out Islands. Some poor Bahamian children live on the Family Islands with their grandparents, while their parents work in Nassau. Their parents send money home and visit on holidays.

People often eat outdoors in the Bahamas.

In many parts of the Bahamas, police officers wear a white shirt and helmet. The design dates back to the time when Great Britain controlled the islands.

People in the Bahamas tend to be upbeat. Everyone from cab drivers and political leaders to police officers and shopkeepers are ready with a smile.

The Bahamas lifestyle is similar to that in the United States and Canada. People in the Bahamas watch the same television shows as people in the United States. Young people talk about the same ball players and admire the same musicians. Yet people on the islands have their own way of doing things—the Bahamas way. And they are proud of that.

Water, Water Everywhere

THE COMMONWEALTH OF THE BAHAMAS IS AN archipelago, or group of islands. It includes 29 major islands, 661 low islands called cays (pronounced KEES), and 2,387 islets, which are hardly more than rocks peeking above the waves. The Bahamas curves in a great arc for 750 miles (1,200 kilometers) in the Atlantic Ocean. The nation's capitol, Nassau, is 244 miles (393 km) north of Cuba and 424 miles (682 km) northwest of the British territories of the Turks and Caicos Islands. The United States is much closer. The Bahamian city of Freeport is only 84 miles (135 km) southeast of Palm Beach, Florida.

Opposite: **The sea is always close by in the Bahamas. No part of the nation is more than about 20 miles (32 km) from the sea.**

The Lay of the Land

The total area of the islands in the Bahamas is only 5,382 square miles (13,939 sq km), about the same size as the U.S. state of Connecticut. Most of the country's 353,658 residents live on New Providence Island. Many of the other islands are home to no one at all. The Bahama Islands are low and flat.

The Bahamas' Geographic Features

Area: 5,382 square miles (13,939 sq km)

Total Coastline: 1,368 miles (3,543 km)

Largest Island: Andros, 2,300 sq miles (6,000 sq km)

Smallest Island: Long Cay, 9 sq miles (23 sq km)

Total Population: 353,658 (2010 est.)

Largest City: Nassau, population 255,789

Least Populated Major Island: Ragged Island, pop. 72

Highest Elevation: Mount Alvernia, 206 feet (63 m) above sea level

Lowest Elevation: Sea level

Average June Temperature: 80°F (27°C)

Average December Temperature: 70°F (21°C)

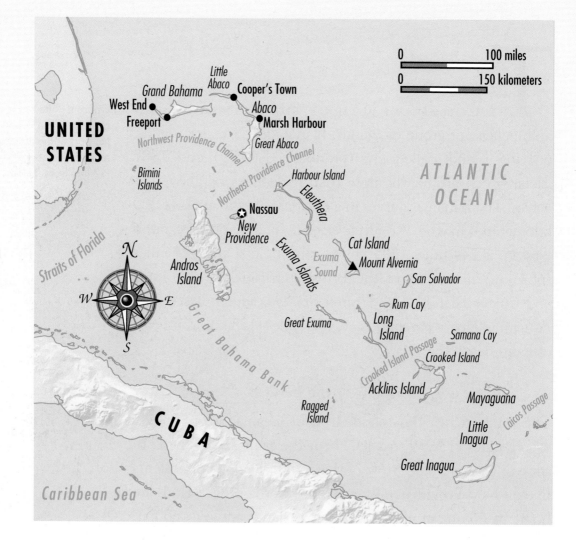

The highest point is a bump on Cat Island. Mount Alvernia rises to only 206 feet (63 meters) above sea level.

The Bahamas are the tips of the Great Bahama Bank and the Little Bahama Bank, stony ridges that rise about 1.5 miles (2.4 km) from the ocean floor. Scientists estimate that it took 104 million years for the ridges to form.

Only a few inches of topsoil covers the islands. Decaying plant material called humus collects in holes in the rock. Farmers use these fertile pits to grow vegetables.

No rivers or streams flow in the Bahamas, but many of the islands do have ponds and swamps. Rainwater filters through

A boardwalk allows visitors to cross a creek in Lucayan National Park on Grand Bahama Island.

Pine forests cover more than half of Grand Bahama Island.

cracks in the ground, collecting in large underground pools. Andros Island receives more rainfall than its neighbors, so its freshwater reservoir is more than 100 feet (30 m) deep. Elsewhere, the pools are only a couple of inches deep. Because freshwater is so valuable, people collect rainwater in barrels.

Northern Islands

The northern part of the Bahamas is not far from Florida. Grand Bahama lies near the northern end of the island nation. The island rises barely 60 feet (18 m) above sea level. It is approximately 93 miles (150 km) long and 12 miles (20 km) wide. Until resort developers arrived in the 1950s and 1960s, Grand Bahama Island was generally laid back and peaceful. It then became a tourist hub.

In 1955, Freeport was established as a free trade zone to encourage business. Companies in Freeport pay no taxes, and the city has become a bustling commercial center. It has factories, oil refineries, and one of the largest deepwater container ports in the world.

The Abaco Islands also lie in the northern part of the Bahamas. Sailors like these islands because they have calm waters and charming ports. Sailors keep an eye out for Hope Town's red and white candy-striped lighthouse, which was built in 1863.

Huge containers are loaded onto ships in Freeport.

Great Abaco is the largest island in the group. On this island is Marsh Harbour, a city of more than six thousand people, which boasts the Abacos' only stoplight. The Abacos are home to several national parks, including Pelican Cays Land and Sea Park, Man of War Cay, and Great Guana Cay. Descendants of horses brought over by early Spanish explorers roam free at the Abaco Wild Horse Preserve.

The Hope Town Lighthouse is one of just three manual lighthouses remaining in the world. It has to be hand cranked every few hours to keep the light flashing at the correct rate.

Looking at the Bahamas' Cities

Nassau is the capital of the Bahamas and its largest city, with a population of 255,789. Freeport (below), the second-largest city, is home to 45,945 people. It was established in 1955, when the government of the Bahamas granted 50,000 acres (20,000 hectares) of land on Grand Bahama Island to a businessman named Wallace Groves to develop economically. Freeport grew into a major tourist center with a major port. Many cruise ships stop there, and visitors enjoy shopping at its markets.

West End (above) is the nation's third-largest city, with 13,577 residents, and is also located on Grand Bahama Island. It is the oldest town on the island. Alcohol was smuggled through West End into the United States during Prohibition in the 1920s, when it was illegal to sell alcohol in the United States. Today, West End is a thriving village full of luxury homes and restaurants.

Cooper's Town, the fourth-largest city, has a population of 9,948 and sits on Abaco Island. It was once an important pineapple-growing region. Today, it is a quiet town near lovely beaches.

Boating is easy on the eastern side of Andros Island but dangerous on the western side because of hidden ridges underwater.

The Bimini Islands, in the northwestern part of the nation, lie closer to Florida than any other Bahamian islands. These tiny islands, which cover only 9 square miles (23 sq km), lie on the edge of the Gulf Stream, a warm, swift ocean current that attracts sea life. The Biminis are renowned for their excellent fishing. In particular, people go there to try to catch large fish such as the sailfish, marlin, and wahoo.

River Under the Sea

The water around the Bahamas is warmed by the Gulf Stream, a swift ocean current much like a warm river flowing through the colder ocean. This water is warmed by the sun in the shallows of the Gulf of Mexico and edges around the tip of Florida. Traveling north up the U.S. coastline, the Gulf Stream enters a deep strait between Florida and the Bahamas. It continues north past Canada before angling east across the Atlantic. The Gulf Stream eventually warms the western European coastline, even helping palm trees grow in Ireland.

Underwater Garden

Some of the world's most beautiful coral reefs are found along the northern rim of the Bahamas. These reefs are made of the skeletal remains of creatures called polyps. When alive, the polyps are a variety of bright reds, greens, and yellows. Each polyp is smaller than a pinhead. They live in shallow, warm oceans where they eat creatures even tinier than they are. Coral reefs are important to the health of ocean life. Fish and many other sea creatures find food and shelter among the corals. The Bahamas Reef Environment Educational Foundation (BREEF) helps preserve these valuable reef ecosystems. It works to establish marine reserves and educate people about the importance of protecting the reefs and sea life.

Central Islands

The largest island in the Bahamas is Andros. It sprawls over 2,300 square miles (6,000 sq km) in the middle of the island chain. It is larger than all the other seven hundred Bahamian islands combined. Andros is split into three major islands—North Andros, Mangrove Cay, and South Andros—and hundreds of islets and cays. The sections of Andros are separated by tidal channels, called bights, which are traveled by ferries, fishing boats, and sailboats.

Andros, which is nicknamed the Big Yard, is home to approximately eight thousand people. Most live along a thin strip of land near the island's eastern coast. The world's third-longest coral reef stretches 142 miles (229 km) off the coast of Andros.

Spanish Wells

Spanish Wells is a village on the small island of St. George's Cay, near the northern end of Eleuthera Island. It was so named because the Spanish dug deep wells there. The wells provided sailors with drinkable water on the difficult journey back to Europe. The strategic harbor later became a haven for the pirates who terrorized the region during the 1700s. Today, divers don't hunt for treasure but for deep-sea crayfish. The fish are caught, cleaned, and frozen before being shipped to gourmet restaurants.

The sands on Harbour Island are pink because they include the crushed shells of tiny creatures called foraminifera.

Around 1648, Captain William Sayle led a group of English settlers from Bermuda to the Bahamas, seeking a place to freely practice their religion. They were shipwrecked on

the north end of a long, skinny island they named Eleutheria, which means "freedom" in Greek. The name later became Eleuthera. The settlers at first held their church services in Preacher's Cave, now a popular tourist site. Today, about eight thousand people live on the island, which lies to the east of Andros. They live in picturesque settlements called Deep Creek, Winding Bay, Savannah Sound, and Gregory Town.

Between Andros and Eleuthera is the small island of New Providence. It is the site of the Bahamas' capital, Nassau. Some 70 percent of the country's population lives in Nassau. They enjoy a fabulous nightlife scene, with clubs, theaters, and restaurants.

Just north of Eleuthera is Harbour Island. It is noted for its pink sand beaches, which are made primarily from the broken shells of microscopic sea creatures called foraminifera. The only settlement on the island is Dunmore Town. In the late 1700s it was the capital of the Bahamas under Lord Dunmore, who was once the country's royal governor.

South of Eleuthera are the Exuma Islands, a group of 365 cays and islands spread over 130 square miles (340 sq km). They are favorites of sailors, who appreciate their quiet coves and beaches. The Exumas have a total population of just 3,500 people. Many of the smaller islands are uninhabited sand dunes or rocky landscapes dotted with saltwater ponds. Others are carpeted in pine forests or thatch palms. The Exuma Cays Land and Sea Park is home to rare rock iguanas that can grow to more than 2 feet long (60 cm). They are nicknamed Bahamian dragons because of their size.

Blue Holes

During the Ice Age, about fifteen thousand years ago, the sea level was much lower than it is today. When the ice melted, the sea level rose. Some land that disappeared beneath the waves eroded easily. In some places, this land collapsed into circular underwater vertical caves. The water in the deep pits looks dark blue, while the shallow water nearby is a much lighter color. Because of this, these pits are called blue holes.

Some blue holes are found inland, while others are offshore. Andros Island has more than two hundred blue holes. On other islands, freshwater bubbles up from cracks in the ocean floor to mingle with the saltwater, creating what are called boiling holes.

Southern Islands

In the southern part of the Bahamas is Long Island, which lives up to its name. This skinny strip of land is 80 miles (130 km) long but barely 4 miles (6 km) wide. The island has many underwater limestone caves, which attract divers seeking excitement. Dean's Blue Hole is the deepest underwater cave in the world, reaching down 663 feet (202 m). Many people consider it one of the world's top places to go swimming. In 2010, William Trubridge broke a world diving record in Dean's Blue Hole. He swam to a depth of 331 feet (101 m) on a single breath of air.

At one time, Long Island's grassy expanse was perfect for raising sheep and cattle. Today, only wild sheep and goats roam there. Most of the island's four thousand residents live near Deadman's Cay, a small town close to a cave system with dazzling limestone formations.

Great Inagua and Little Inagua, the southernmost islands of the Bahamas, are the hottest and driest of the islands. Only about 970 people live on Great Inagua, while Little Inagua is populated only by herds of wild donkeys and goats. Great Inagua's capital, Matthew Town, produces 1 million tons of sea salt annually for the Morton Salt Company. Half of Great

Little Inagua's wild donkeys are the descendants of animals brought to the Bahamas by the French.

Inagua is a bird sanctuary, home to hummingbirds, pelicans, flamingos, egrets, and other species. Sixty thousand West Indian flamingos live on Great Inagua. It is the world's largest flock of flamingos.

Isles of June

Winds blow continuously across the Bahamas, creating gentle, balmy weather. The average summer temperature is 80 degrees Fahrenheit (27 degrees Celsius), while the usual winter temperature hovers around 70°F (21°C). Temperatures tend to be a bit cooler on the northern islands during the winter. People wear sweaters or jackets to ward off the chill.

Tourists love coming to the Bahamas between September and May, when it might be snowy or rainy where they live. This is when the Bahamas lives up to its nickname, the Isles of June, because the weather is so pleasant. Rarely does the temperature rise above 90°F (32°C) or drop below 60°F (16°C). The skies are mostly clear. In fact, the nation averages 310 sunny days a year.

Still, it often rains from May through September. Nassau averages 55 inches (140 centimeters) of rain per year. Rain most often falls in the morning and midafternoon. The thundershowers clear quickly, so Bahamians rarely worry about carrying umbrellas.

Howling Hurricanes

Hurricanes are powerful storms that sweep across the ocean between June and November. Their fierce winds can reach up to 150 miles per hour (240 kph).

Satellites track the storms as they move across the ocean, so people usually find out about upcoming weather with plenty of time to take cover. Bahamians have built seawalls to help blunt the force of the waves churned by the wind. But sometimes even these safeguards are not enough. Hurricanes occasionally rip roofs off buildings, tear down power lines, uproot trees, crumple buildings, and take lives. For more than twelve hours on September 13 and 14, 1999, the winds of Hurricane Floyd were clocked at about 155 miles per hour (249 kph). Fifty-foot (15 m) waves crashed ashore, devastating Eleuthera and Abaco Islands. People were without food, water, and electricity for days.

Storms frequently blow across the Bahamas.

Glorious Life

S TROLLING ALONG THE BACK ROADS OF THE Bahamas, the air is thick with the scent of hibiscus and frangipani. Even people in boats offshore can sometimes enjoy the windblown fragrance.

In the Bahamas, pockets of fertile soil and a moderate climate lead to abundant vegetation. Different plants thrive in different parts of the Bahamas. The northern islands receive up to three times as much rain as the southern islands, so they tend to have more flowers and forests. Stands of Caribbean pine carpet Grand Bahama and Andros, while sharp-spiked cacti are common on Inagua.

Tree Varieties

More than fifty types of trees grow in the Bahamas. The Caribbean pine grows across the northern and central islands. Its wood has often been used to build homes and ships.

The Bahamas also has many varieties of palm trees. The cabbage palmetto grows where there is a lot of freshwater, and the

Opposite: **The showy hibiscus flower blooms year-round in the Bahamas. Its large petals are edible.**

thatch palm grows in drier areas. Coconut palms are not native to the Bahamas. However, they are among the most valuable plants in the Bahamas. Their fronds can be used to make roofs, or they can be woven into hats. The coconuts are often used in cooking. Bahamian cooks use coconut in tarts, cakes, and ice cream, and shredded coconut is added to almost anything. Coconuts are celebrated with a huge festival in July on South Andros Island.

Mangrove trees are unusual because they can grow in saltwater. Ocean water will kill most trees. Red mangrove trees thrive in shallow swamps. Some red mangroves grow just 5 feet (1.5 m) tall, while others soar to 20 feet (6 m) in height. Stands of black mangrove trees are found in deeper water. The mangroves are full of nutrients, and their roots provide shelter for fish. The brackish (salty) lakes on San Salvador are perfect for mangroves.

In recent decades, many mangrove forests have been cut down to make room for resorts, harbors, and homes. This wor-

National Tree

The lignum vitae, the national tree of the Bahamas, grows mostly on the southern islands. When the tree is in bloom, delicate purple flowers peek out from amid its olive-green leaves. Lignum vitae grows slowly and can live more then a century.

Locals call the lignum vitae ironwood because it is one of the hardest woods in the world. Long ago, shipbuilders learned that lignum vitae is not good for making boats. It is so dense it will not float. Instead, the oily wood is used to make fine furniture or parts for ship propellers.

Small fish find shelter among the roots of mangrove trees.

ries many people. The mangroves help keep fish populations healthy because baby fish find safety among the trees' roots. The trees also help protect the land from storms. Without the trees and their extensive root system protecting the shoreline, heavy rain and crashing waves can more easily wash away the land. The country takes these issues seriously. It has established preserves, such as Inagua National Park, to help protect these mangrove forests.

Towering breadfruit trees shade Nassau's streets. The tallest ones reach 85 feet (26 m) high. The tree's delicious fruit is often used to make soup. Bahamians also sometimes rub toasted breadfruit flowers on their gums to soothe toothaches.

National Flower

Bahamians chose the yellow elder as their national flower in the 1970s. The small trees produce tubular golden flowers that have intricate red stripes on each petal. They bloom from October to December.

Many trees in the Bahamas produce showy blossoms. One of the most magnificent flowering trees is the pink poui, which produces huge clusters of bright, trumpet-shaped flowers. The red bottlebrush tree produces long, thin blooms that stick straight out and look just like a bottlebrush.

The bottlebrush tree produces flower spikes that are up to 4 inches (10 cm) long.

Brilliant Flowers

Many smaller plants also produce gorgeous flowers. There are many different forms of frangipani. Some are trees, while others are smaller shrubs. Because of its beautiful and long-lived blooms, frangipani is often planted near churches and cemeteries, earning it the nickname the Temple Tree. The sweet-smelling frangipani is more fragrant at night and comes in a variety of colors, including white, yellow, pink, and red.

Hibiscus grows throughout the islands. Although these glamorous flowers explode in every color imaginable, red and pink are the most common. Hibiscus flowers, which bloom year-round, are also delicious to eat. They are used to decorate salads or are brewed into tea.

The sea grape produces rows of white blooms. The plant's sweet fruit is used to make a delicious jam. The fast-growing allamanda boasts yellow trumpet-shaped flowers. The plant grows in ditches and backyards, particularly on Abaco. Children know to be careful of it because its milky sap is poisonous and causes blisters and rashes on the skin.

Plants from Afar

Over thousands of years, the wind and waves have carried seeds about, bringing new plant species to the islands. Gardeners and farmers have also brought plants from other countries. One common nonnative species in the Bahamas is the crepe myrtle. Originally from Asia, this beautiful plant has pink flower clusters 4 to 9 inches (10 to 23 cm) long.

Bougainvillea is the plant most commonly grown in the Bahamas for its beauty. Its vivid purples and reds peek out from behind fences and along highways. Also common is the passionflower, a climbing plant that crawls over shrubs, up trees, and along walls.

Under the Sea

The oceans around the Bahamas also support plant life. Star grass grows as deep as 130 feet (40 m) below the water's surface in either mud or sand. Dense beds of manatee grass grow in warm, shallow waters.

Many creatures also live beneath the waves. Coral found in the region includes delicate sea fans, elkhorn coral, and brain coral. They live in colonies made up of many individuals called polyps. The coral reefs provide homes and food for spiny lobster, conch, grouper, and snapper, and many other

Creating Reefs

Coral reefs are vital homes for sea creatures, but they are also delicate and easily damaged. To help sea life thrive, people sometimes create artificial reefs where sea creatures can find food and shelter. Old ships that are no longer sailed are often used to make the reefs. A freighter, known as *Theo's Wreck*, was deliberately sunk off Grand Bahama in 1982. It is now a fish hotel at the edge of the Grand Bahama Ledge, a 2,000-foot (610 m) drop to the ocean's dark basement. More recently, the Royal Caribbean cruise line has been helping construct concrete reefs off Coco Cay, a resort island northwest of Andros.

types of sea life. But the reefs are delicate and easily damaged by overfishing, pollution, and ships dragging their anchors.

The barracuda is a fast swimmer. When chasing prey, it can reach 36 miles per hour (58 kph).

Fish

Many kinds of fish swim off the coast of the Bahamas. Fishers seek yellowtail snappers, blue-striped grunts, parrot fish, Nassau groupers, bonefish, feisty tarpons, and toothy barracudas. Sharks, queen triggerfish, turbot, porkfish, goatfish, and dozens of other species also glide through the warm water. Stingrays have a huge, flapping body that enables them to float along lazily or hurry when chased by a predator.

Some of the Bahamas' most unusual fish live in a cave at the ocean's edge on Eleuthera. This cave is a haven for tiny,

Sharks in the Bahamas

Forty species of sharks swim in the waters around the Bahamas. The hammerhead shark can reach lengths of up to 18 feet (6 m). It feeds on small bony fish or stingrays. The bulky tiger shark is noted for the distinctive stripes along its sides. It can be found in shallow water, nibbling on everything from turtles to other sharks. The Caribbean reef shark is usually gray with a white underbelly and a short blunt snout.

Nurse sharks usually rest on the ocean floor during the day and hunt at night, munching on shrimp, octopuses, and crabs. The whitetip shark is usually escorted by pilot fish, which gobble leftovers and eat parasites on the sharks' bodies.

Because of a worldwide decline in shark populations, shark fishing was banned in the Bahamas as of 2011. The nation's territorial waters are now a shark sanctuary.

blind fish. Their ancestors were trapped in the cave long ago. Over the generations, they adapted to life in the permanent darkness, where eyesight is not useful.

Bird Life

At least four bird species can be found only in the Bahamas: the Bahama woodstar, the white-cheeked (or Bahama) pintail, the Bahama swallow, and the Bahama yellowthroat. Other birds living among the mangroves are the spotted sandpiper, roseate spoonbill, green heron, belted kingfisher, mangrove warbler, and reddish egret. The national bird is the flamingo.

When Christopher Columbus visited the Bahamas, he noted thick flocks of parrots. There were so many parrots that they blocked the sun. Today, the only remaining parrots live on Abaco and Great Inagua Islands. These parrots nest on the ground, making them an easy target for feral, or wild, cats. In 2004, the parrot population suffered greatly from a forest fire and, not long after that, a hurricane. Conservation groups are currently working to save the parrots.

Island Animals

Thirty-two types of mammals can be found in the Bahamas. The Bahamian hutia is about the size of a small rabbit but looks like a

An estimated three thousand parrots live in the Bahamas.

gopher. Protected by the Wild Animals Protection Act of 1968, the plump little hutia lives in brushy areas of New Providence and Grand Bahama Islands. Hutias scurry around at night munching on leaves and twigs. The funnel-eared bat can be found on San Salvador Island and seen at Thunderball Grotto on Great Exuma and Hatchet Bay Cave on Eleuthera. To see the bats, it's best to go in the daytime, when they are asleep—hanging upside down.

Some mammals in the Bahamas are not native to the islands. Explorers and early settlers brought animals that eventually became pests. These include horses, donkeys, goats, hogs, raccoons, and rats.

The islands' amphibians include squirrel tree frogs, pig frogs, southern leopard frogs, and narrow-mouthed toads. The nation's reptiles include sea turtles and eight varieties of Bahamian boa constrictors. These snakes, which lunch on frogs, birds, and rats, live on all the major islands except Grand Bahama and San Salvador.

Sea Turtles

Five species of graceful sea turtles live in the waters near the Bahamas. The smallest is the Kemp's ridley turtle, which weighs less than 100 pounds (45 kg). The leatherback turtle can sometimes reach 1,300 pounds (590 kg). In the middle in size are the hawksbill (right), loggerhead, and green turtles. Female turtles come ashore to lay their eggs in the sand. The tiny hatchlings struggle back to the water where they grow to adulthood. The Bahamas Sea Turtle Conservation Group helps ensure that the nesting grounds are protected.

Protecting Wildlife

The Bahamas has set aside a number of areas where animal life is vigorously protected. In 1958, the Exuma Cays Land and Sea Park was established as the first national park in the Bahamas. The park protects delicate ecosystems, such as coral reefs and sandbars, and many endangered species, including the Bahamian hutia, the sooty tern, and the rock iguana.

In 2002, the park system doubled in size. Ten new parks were created to safeguard both marine and land regions. The largest park is Central Andros National Park at 286,080 acres (115,772 ha). The smallest is the windswept 1.5-acre (0.6 ha) Peterson Cay preserve on Grand Bahama. Fossils of ancient plant and animal life have been found in the 7.5-acre (3 ha) Primeval Forest National Park on New Providence.

The Allen's Cay rock iguana is severely endangered. Only about a thousand survive in the wild.

The Old Days

IMAGINE HOW SURPRISED THE LUCAYAN PEOPLE MUST have been in 1492 when they saw a European for the first time. Explorer Christopher Columbus had just arrived on the island of San Salvador. With the simple act of stepping out of a rowboat onto the sand, Columbus set history on a new course.

Columbus was one of a small band of adventurers exploring the world during what is sometimes called the Age of Discovery. In the 1300s and 1400s, the kings of Europe were eager to fill their treasuries and expand their territories. They also wanted to trade for spices, silks, and other valuable goods with merchants in the Indies, in the Far East. But long, overland trade routes were slow and dangerous. Explorers set off to find a better route. Columbus, a well-known trader from Italy, believed he could get to the Indies by sailing west.

With funding from the Spanish crown, Columbus and his crew sailed off in his small boats, the *Santa María*, the *Niña*, and the *Pinta*. They departed in August 1492. The weeks went by with no sight of land, and the crew became

Opposite: **Christopher Columbus and his crew arrived in the Bahamas on October 12, 1492.**

discouraged. But on October 12, a lookout aboard the *Pinta* thought he saw something in the distance. Looking hard, he spotted the white blur of sand dunes reflected in the moonlight. Columbus and the crew anchored their ships and went ashore. Wading through the surf, Columbus called their discovery *gran bajamar*, meaning "great shallows." Over the years, this term evolved into "the Bahamas."

Lucayan Life

Columbus thought he had reached the Indies, so he called the people who were living on the island Indians. In fact, they were the Lucayan, a branch of the Taino people who lived

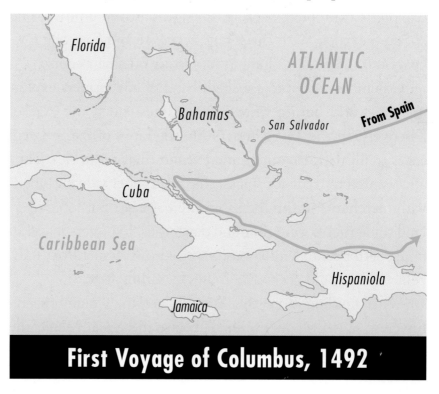

First Voyage of Columbus, 1492

throughout the Caribbean. The Lucayan people had been living in the Bahamas for centuries. They probably arrived there between 500 and 800 CE. They likely first settled the southern part of the Bahamas and slowly spread across the island chain.

The Lucayans lived in round houses made of poles with thatched roofs. The Lucayans grew crops, most commonly a root vegetable called manioc. They fished, gathered wild foods such as guava fruit, and hunted animals such as iguanas, hutias, and land crabs.

A replica of a Lucayan village has been built on San Salvador. The Lucayan people lived in houses made of twigs and thatched roofs.

Meeting the Europeans

The Spanish called the people of the Bahamas Lucayos. The Bahamians called themselves Lukku-cairi, which means "people of the islands."

After Columbus and his men waded ashore, the Lucayans slowly emerged to greet them. They brought parrots and other gifts to the newcomers.

Columbus did not stay long on San Salvador. He was eager to make more discoveries, and soon returned to Spain with news of what he had found. He later made three more trips across the Atlantic.

The Lucayans suffered terribly as other Europeans arrived in the Bahamas. An estimated forty thousand Lucayans were enslaved by the Europeans and forced to work in mines on the island of Hispaniola, which is now the location of the nations of Haiti and the Dominican Republic. Once all these people were uprooted, the Bahamas was almost empty. In 1520, the Spanish decided to remove the last remaining Lucayans from the Bahamas. There were only eleven still there.

Sir Robert Heath (left) was the attorney general (the chief legal adviser) to King Charles I. The king gave Heath control of the Bahamas.

For the next century, no one showed much interest in the Bahamas. But in 1629, King Charles I of England gave permission for Sir Robert Heath to establish colonies in the Carolinas, along the east coast of North America. He also gave Heath rights to the Bahamas. But Heath did not settle the islands.

In the 1640s, England was in the midst of a civil war as Puritans split away from the Anglican Church. This civil war spilled over to the colonies. A group of settlers on the island of Bermuda, located about 580 miles (930 km) from the North American coastline, wanted to worship as they pleased.

Led by Captain William Sayle, these self-described Adventurers left Bermuda around 1648. But they were shipwrecked off the island of Eleuthera and decided to stay. This became the first permanent European settlement in the Bahamas. After their farms failed, the Adventurers cut timber to be sold or traded for food to other Puritan communities. Supplies were sent from Massachusetts to help the struggling Bahamas colony.

In 1656, another group of Puritans settled on New Providence Island. It was named after Providence Island, off the coast of Nicaragua, which earlier Puritans had tried to settle. But New Providence was hard to protect and too far away to easily receive supplies. So this experiment failed. By 1670, barely a thousand Puritans remained in the Bahamas.

Also in 1670, a group of well-to-do English businessmen, called the lords proprietors, were granted royal approval to colonize the Bahamas. But they paid little attention to the islands and left them alone.

Dangerous Years

Although religious groups had difficulty establishing themselves in the Bahamas, pirates thrived. In the seventeenth century, Spanish treasure ships on their way home from South America were often attacked by pirates.

French pirates board a Spanish ship. An estimated one thousand pirates roamed the Bahamas in 1713.

The Bahamas made a perfect pirate base. Both the English and the French governments protected the pirates. The English and French wanted to harass their enemies, such as the Spanish, without sending their own troops to do it. The pirates served this purpose. The English king knighted a pirate named Henry Morgan for his bold raids on the Spanish. Morgan's Bluff on Andros Island is named after him.

The pirates often swarmed out to attack passing victims. Some were "wreckers," who lured their prey onto the reefs. When the vessels smashed on the rocks, the looters helped themselves to whatever cargo washed ashore. The pirates hid out in the snug harbor in Nassau, which was then called Charles Town. The Spanish wanted to protect their sea routes so they attacked and destroyed the city in 1684.

The British government was growing tired of the pirates. In 1717, the lords proprietors returned control of the Bahamas to the British government. The following year, Woodes Rogers

Legendary Lives

The exploits of the pirates have become legendary. A watchtower overlooking Nassau is now a crumbling ruin. Supposedly, it was used by Edward Teach, the fearsome pirate known as Blackbeard. He tied slow-burning hemp to his hat and beard so smoke would circle his head, making him appear more frightening when he was fighting. Not all pirates were men. Red-haired Anne Bonny and fiery Mary Read fought alongside pirate Calico Jack Rackham. They fired pistols and wielded swords as well as, if not better than, any man.

was named the royal governor. He vowed to clean up the Bahamas colony. His motto was Piracy Expelled, Commerce Restored. Under his leadership, many pirates were captured. Some were hanged in Nassau's main square.

Changing Populations

When the American Revolution broke out in 1775, the Bahamas was an important British outpost. A number of wealthy colonial families loyal to the king fled to the Bahamas when the gunfire started. Some private individuals acted almost like pirates. These "privateers" raided American and Spanish ships with permission from the British.

Warships from both America and Spain attacked Nassau in an attempt to stop the raids. American vessels sailed into the city's harbor in 1776 and again in 1778, but did little damage. Spanish forces took control of the islands in May 1782. A year later, Colonel Andrew Deveaux led a group of Loyalists, supporters of the British during the war, in successfully retaking the country.

A statue of Woodes Rogers stands in Nassau. He served two terms as governor of the Bahamas.

Workers plant sugarcane on a farm in the Bahamas.

Following the American victory in the revolution, more Loyalists fled to the Bahamas from the mainland. Almost ten thousand Loyalists sailed to the Bahamas, mostly to the Abacos.

Many of the newcomers brought slaves with them. Before this influx, there were probably fewer than one thousand enslaved people in the Bahamas. Thousands more came with the Loyalists. They worked on cotton plantations on Crooked Island, cut timber on Andros, and labored in salt mines on Great Inagua.

The Bahamas was on the slave trade shipping route between Africa and North America, so slave markets were active there. Plantation owners felt that black Africans could work longer and harder under the searing Bahamian sun than other people could. Under the slave system, even girls as young as four years old worked on estates, helping women wash clothes and cook. By the time they were twelve, children were sent into the fields to work from dawn to dusk.

Not all black Bahamians were enslaved. But none were allowed to vote until 1807. Four black Bahamians were members of the Bahamian Assembly in 1834. In that year, Britain ended slavery throughout its empire, including the Bahamas. Under a new law, owners had to provide their former slaves with an apprenticeship program. The newly freed people were to be trained in jobs and were not to work more than forty-

The market in Nassau in 1856

five hours a week, in addition to being fed and clothed. The apprenticeship program ended in 1838.

A Growing Economy

The Bahamian economy boomed during the U.S. Civil War from 1861 to 1865. Union gunboats had blockaded some Southern cities, so ships carrying food and other supplies could not dock. The islanders became expert at blockade running.

Bahamian blockade runners slipped into Charleston, South Carolina, at night and loaded their ships with cotton. They then made the two-day trip back to the Bahamas (below) where they traded the cotton for British goods.

They slipped ships past Union gunboats to smuggle food and medicine to the Confederates in exchange for cotton. This economic bubble burst when the war ended.

By the beginning of the twentieth century, collecting sea sponges and growing pineapples were the mainstays of the Bahamian economy. This ended, however, when both products could be obtained cheaper elsewhere. Eager for jobs, one in five Bahamians left the islands, heading to Florida's citrus groves as seasonal laborers.

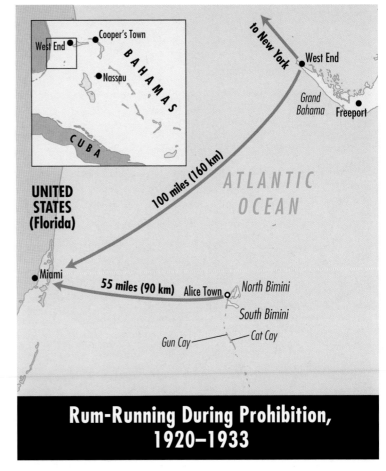

Rum-Running During Prohibition, 1920–1933

The United States outlawed the manufacture and sale of alcohol in 1919 beginning what is known as Prohibition. Commerce once more boomed in the Bahamas. During Prohibition, smugglers called rumrunners flitted in and out of Gun Cay, Cat Cay, Bimini, and West End. Their small, swift motorboats easily crossed the 60 miles (100 km) of choppy ocean to Florida's beaches. Some of the illegal liquor was then moved to larger ships for transport farther up the U.S. coastline. During this time, the Bahamas was awash in cash. The government collected millions of dollars in taxes on every bottle that flowed through Nassau's port.

A sponge merchant sorts through a huge pile of sponges. Selling sponges was once an important source of income for the Bahamas.

Prohibition ended in 1933, and along with it the rum-running business. By that time, however, the Bahamas had already begun turning to other endeavors, particularly tourism.

Collapse and Recovery

In the late 1920s, a worldwide economic collapse called the Great Depression began. It would last throughout the 1930s. Like other people around the globe, Bahamians also suffered. Hundreds lost their savings as banks failed. Meanwhile, a disease devastated the sponge industry, causing many Bahamians to lose their jobs.

These setbacks did not faze businesspeople such as local real estate developer Harold Christie and Canadian millionaire Harry Oakes. They became the most powerful men in the country, snapping up acres of land on New Providence to build hotels, hospitals, golf courses, and houses. Their projects helped jump-start the economy. By the time World War II began in 1939, the country was getting back on its financial feet. The activity at American and British air force bases in the Bahamas during the war also helped the economy.

As the 1940s ended, tourism regained its position as the islands' most important industry. Americans flocked to the Bahamas for vacations. In 1957, a former wartime airfield was turned into Nassau's international airport. By the 1960s, the nation had also become an international financial center. Corporations set up there because they did not have to pay any taxes if they had an office in the Bahamas.

Women sell baskets to tourists in Nassau in 1955.

The Father of the Bahamas

Lynden O. Pindling (1930–2000) was prime minister of the Bahamas from 1967 to 1992 and is considered the Father of the Bahamas. Pindling grew up in Nassau, where his father was a constable in the Royal Bahamas Police Force. Pindling became a bank clerk and then a lawyer before entering politics. By 1965, he had become the leader of the Progressive Liberal Party. Pindling led his country to independence from Great Britain in 1973 and was knighted by Queen Elizabeth II in 1983.

Yet while the rich got richer, many Bahamians did not share in the wealth. Subsequently, there were strikes and street marches by people seeking better wages and working hours.

Independence

The postwar era saw a rise in political activity as well. A group of white business leaders nicknamed the Bay Street Boys had been running the country from behind the scenes. They organized the United Bahamian Party to safeguard their social status and financial power. Some black Bahamians also belonged to the United Bahamian Party. The other major political party, the Progressive Liberal Party, was made up of black, multiracial, and progressive white Bahamians. In 1964, after more than two centuries of being a British colony, constitutional changes were negotiated at a conference in London, England. Sir Roland T. Symonette, a member of the United Bahamian Party, became the first premier of the Bahamas under a new constitution. A bicameral, or two-house, legislature was also established.

Full internal self-government was achieved with the signing of a 1969 constitution, which changed the colony's name to the Commonwealth of the Bahamas. However, the nation was still not totally independent of Britain. A constitutional conference was held in 1972, opening the way for true national independence. After much discussion and many compromises, a new independence constitution was written. On behalf of Queen Elizabeth II, on July 10, 1973, Prince Charles of Britain presented the independence constitution to Bahamian prime minister Lynden O. Pindling. At midnight, the British flag over Nassau's Fort Charlotte was lowered and put away forever. With the new Bahamian flag in its place, the Bahamas was finally a sovereign country.

British and Bahamian officials met in 1972 to discuss Bahamian independence.

Running the Government

THE BAHAMAS IS A DEMOCRATIC NATION. IT HOLDS peaceful elections for its leaders and has a strong constitution that protects many rights of its citizens. They can speak freely, practice whatever religion they want to, and keep their privacy. The nation's constitution was adopted in 1973 when the Bahamas became independent from Great Britain. Parliament can change the constitution, but those changes must be approved by a vote of the people before they can take effect.

The Bahamas retains close ties to its former "mother country" as a member of the British Commonwealth. The commonwealth is a group of countries that once belonged to Britain, whose monarch, or ruler, acts as head of state. This is a ceremonial position with no real power. Elizabeth II has held that post since she became queen in 1952.

Opposite: **Perry Christie (center) was sworn in as prime minister in May 2012.**

The Executive Branch

Queen Elizabeth II appoints a governor-general who represents the British Crown's interests in the Bahamas. Sir Milo B. Butler, who took office in 1973, was the first governor-general who

National Government of the Bahamas

Executive Branch

BRITISH MONARCH

GOVERNOR-GENERAL

PRIME MINISTER

CABINET

Legislative Branch

SENATE

HOUSE OF ASSEMBLY

Judicial Branch

PRIVY COUNCIL

COURT OF APPEAL

SUPREME COURT

MAGISTRATE COURTS

had been born in the Bahamas. In 2010, Sir Arthur Alexander Foulkes became governor-general.

The real head of government is the prime minister, who is the leader of the majority political party. The prime minister leads a group of ministers called the cabinet. Perry Christie became prime minister in 2012. He also served as prime minister from 2002 to 2007. Each of the other ministers is responsible for a specific government department, such as education, tourism, environment, or welfare. In 2012, there were thirteen cabinet posts, along with a deputy prime minister and the attorney general.

The Legislative Branch

A legislative body for the Bahamas first met in 1729. It was called the General Assembly and consisted of twenty-four members representing New Providence, Eleuthera, and

The Bahamian Parliament meets in this building in Nassau.

National Flag

The Bahamas has flown its own national flag since independence from Britain in 1973. It consists of a black triangle and a horizontal gold stripe between two aquamarine stripes. The black triangle, which is at the mast, symbolizes the power and energy of the nation's citizens. The gold stripe in the middle represents the sun, while the two aquamarine stripes stand for the islands' surrounding oceans.

Harbour Islands. Today, the country has a two-house parliament made up of a Senate and a House of Assembly. They meet in distinctive pink buildings in Parliament Square in the capital city of Nassau.

The senators, which number sixteen, are appointed by the governor-general. Of these sixteen senators, nine are appointed based on the prime minister's advice, four based on the advice of the leader of the party that is not in power (the opposition), and three based on the mutual agreement of the prime minister and the opposition party leader. All senators serve five-year terms.

Members of the assembly are elected. In 2012, there were thirty-eight representatives. The number can change depending on the recommendation of the Constituencies Commission, which reviews electoral district boundaries at least every five years.

To pass a law, a bill is introduced in the House of Assembly, read three times, and debated. If it passes, the act is also read three times in the Senate and then sent to the governor-general. He or she signs the act into law.

Nassau: The Center of the Nation

Nassau, the capital of the Bahamas, is located on New Providence Island. In 2012, it was home to an estimated 255,789 people, or about 70 percent of the country's population. Nassau was called Charles Town when it was built in 1670. It was destroyed by the Spanish in 1684, but later rebuilt. Its name was changed to Nassau in 1695 to honor William III, who had been the prince of Orange-Nassau in the Netherlands before becoming king of England in 1689.

Nassau is the center of Bahamian business, industry, and politics. The soft pink buildings housing the country's parliament and Supreme Court are found in the historical center of town, shaded by lovely palm trees and surrounded by fragrant flowers. More than four hundred banks and trust companies are also located here. Men and women in business clothes hurry along Bay Street and Woodes Rogers Walk as they head to meetings. Meanwhile, tourists in shorts and T-shirts take their time visiting the Pirates of Nassau Museum and Christ Church Cathedral. They browse souvenir shops and haggle over the prices of baskets and hats in the Straw Market.

Nassau's many attractions include Fort Fincastle (below, right), which was built in 1793. Shaped like the bow of a ship, the towering stone walls of the fort command the view from atop Bennet's Hill, the highest point on the island at 200 feet (60 m) above sea level. The sixty-five steps of the Queen's Staircase leading to the fort were carved out of solid limestone in the late eighteenth century.

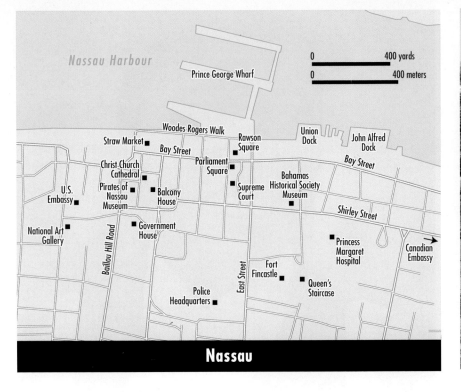

Nassau

In the Bahamas, the judicial branch is independent of executive control, meaning it isn't influenced by other branches of the government. Trials and investigations are held in the nation's magistrate courts. They also handle cases involving young people and family disputes. The next highest court is the Supreme Court, which consists of twelve justices appointed by the governor-general. The Supreme Court reviews decisions from lower courts.

The highest court in the land is the Court of Appeal, which

Judges on the Supreme Court and the Court of Appeal wear traditional wigs and gowns.

The National Anthem

"March On, Bahamaland" was adopted as the national anthem of the Bahamas in 1973. Timothy Gibson wrote the words and music.

Lift up your head to the rising sun, Bahamaland,
March on to glory, your bright banners waving high.
See how the world marks the manner of your bearing!
Pledge to excel through love and unity.
Pressing onward, march together, to a common loftier goal;
Steady sunward though the weather hide the wide and treacherous shoal.
Lift up your head to the rising sun, Bahamaland.
Till the road you've trod lead unto your God,
March on, Bahamaland!

has six members. If needed, a final appeal may be made to the Judicial Committee of Her Majesty's Privy Council in London.

International Efforts

The Bahamas works with many nations to improve global situations. During an uprising to protest restrictive military rule in Haiti in 1994, the Bahamas supplied officers to a military force of many nations that helped restore civilian rule. Law enforcement officials from the Bahamas and the United States work closely to halt the illegal flow of immigrants and drugs from the islands to the North American mainland. In addition, Bahamians often take the lead in the region's social, business, security, and financial activities as active members of the International Red Cross, the Caribbean Community, the International Maritime Organization, and the Organization of American States.

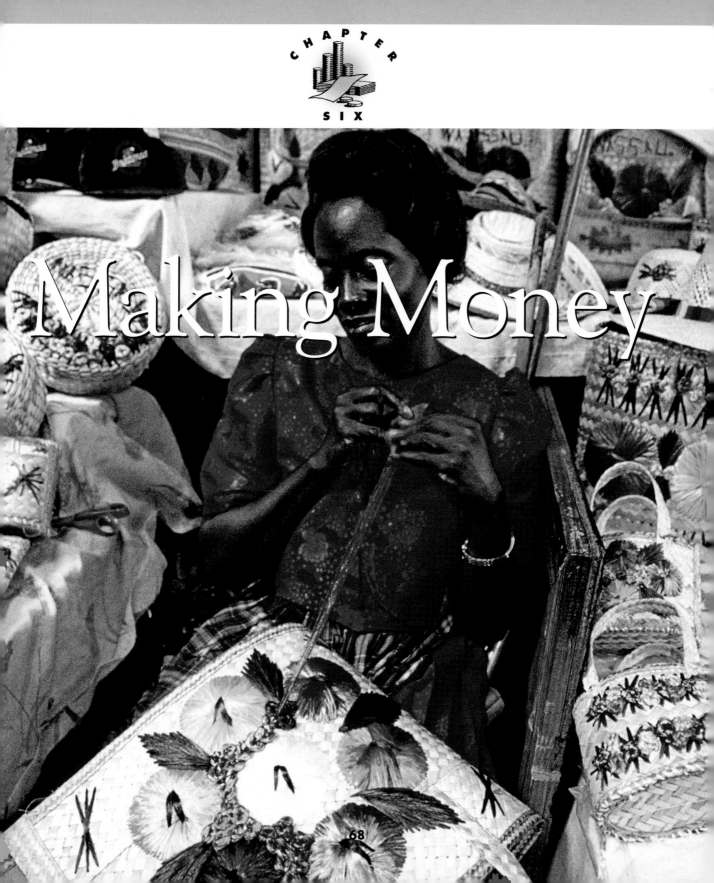

CHAPTER SIX

Making Money

The Bahamas is a wealthy country, with an economy heavily dependent on tourism and banking. It was not always so prosperous, however. Over the years, many Bahamians had to migrate elsewhere to find jobs. Thousands became sailors aboard freighters hauling cargo to far-off ports. Others were contract workers, hired out for months at a time to help dig the Panama Canal, cut timber in Central America, lay railroad tracks in Mexico, or harvest oranges in the United States. These hard-working Bahamians sent their wages back home to support their families.

Opposite: **A basket maker decorates baskets to sell to tourists at the Straw Market in Nassau.**

Tourism and Other Services

Today, tourism along with tourism-related construction, such as the building of water parks and golf courses, make up approximately 60 percent of the gross domestic product (GDP). This is the total value of all the goods and services produced in the country in one year.

Start Small, Grow Large

In 1955, an important piece of legislation was named after a small inlet on Grand Bahama Island. The Hawksbill Creek Agreement created a duty-free zone on the island. As a result, the city of Freeport was built.

Businesses can store or assemble goods there without paying taxes until they ship their products. This saves them money and makes it profitable for them to be located in the Bahamas.

Tourism directly or indirectly employs half of the nation's workforce, which includes almost 190,000 people. If tourists did not come to the Bahamas and spend their money, many cooks, waiters, taxi drivers, and shopkeepers would not be able to pay their bills. They would not be able to buy food and clothes, or pay their rent. So, almost everyone is happy to see the flood of visitors stepping off cruise ships at Prince George Wharf Cruise Terminal or flying into one of the country's airports.

In 2010, of the five million tourists who visited the Bahamas, around 80 percent were from the United States. The following year, a comfortable new terminal at the Nassau airport was completed to accommodate the many arrivals from the United States.

The Bahamas is always working to increase services for its guests, often with the

Each year, more than 1,800 cruise ships arrive in the Bahamas.

help of other nations. The Export-Import Bank of China provided much of the several billion dollars needed to build the Baha Mar resort on Nassau's Cable Beach. Scheduled to open in 2014, the property will feature the largest casino in the Caribbean, convention and meeting facilities, three spas, a golf course, and lovely beaches.

Visitors come to the Bahamas in search of relaxation and sunshine.

Longtime Tourist Haven

Peter Henry Bruce, an English military engineer, was sent to the Bahamas in 1740 to repair Nassau's forts. Overwhelmed by the beauty and warm climate of the islands, he noted that the Bahamas could be used to help the sick recover from their illnesses.

In 1859, a paddle wheel steamship called the *Karnak* made the first trip between New York and Nassau. Two years later, the Royal Victoria Hotel

opened. Its rooms were quickly occupied by the era's rich and famous. By 1925, cruise ships were leaving the United States, Great Britain, and Canada and heading to the Bahamas. Sportfishing, swimming, and golf attracted visitors to the islands in the 1930s.

By 1950, thirty-two thousand tourists arrived in the Bahamas every year. Today, this number is more than five million.

Visitors to the Bahamas can choose among hundreds of hotels and resorts.

Not everyone is happy with the emphasis the nation places on tourism. Some Bahamians believe that tourism has led to an increase in crime, overcrowded cities, rising pollution levels, and a strain on water and electrical systems in urban areas. Yet even with these challenges, tourism is expected to remain the most important contributor to the islands' strong economy.

Financial services are the second most important part of the Bahamian economy. Many corporations locate offices in the country because the tax rate in the Bahamas is lower than the U.S. tax rate. They also appreciate that the Bahamas is a stable democracy, is close to the United States, and has a deep pool of skilled professional workers.

Manufacturing and Mining

Manufacturing and agriculture are important in the Bahamas, but neither has shown much growth in recent years, despite government incentives to make it easier for companies to locate there. Large and small electrical and pharmaceutical manufacturers have discovered the advantages of working

Salt of the Earth

Mining salt has a long history in the Bahamas. Salt was likely an important trade item among the Lucayans hundreds of years ago. In the late 1600s, Bermudans began looking for salt in the Bahamas. They harvested the salt in

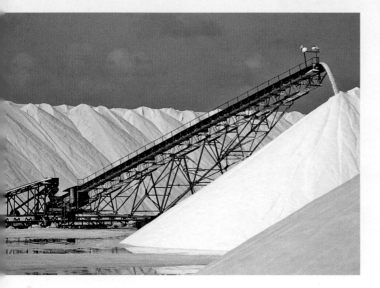

shallow lakes on several islands and then sold it to passing ships. The lack of rainfall to dilute the salt made it high quality, especially on Great Inagua. The first corporation in the Bahamas was the Henagua Salt Pond Company. Formed in 1849, it established the salt industry on Great Inagua. The industry slumped during World War I, but in 1936, the Erickson brothers of Massachusetts revived it. The giant Morton Salt Company later bought the Erickson firm. Today, Morton maintains 2,279 acres (922 ha) of salt ponds on Great Inagua, producing more than one million tons of salt annually.

To collect the salt, seawater is pumped into shallow pools where it mostly evaporates, a process helped along by the soft ocean breeze. Through a gradual process of being moved to another pool and then another, impurities are eventually separated out from the salt. Any remaining liquid is pumped away. Bulldozers then push the salt into towering mounds to await shipment overseas.

in the Bahamas. Beer and alcohol makers are also important employers in the area. Other important businesses include producing sun-dried sea salt in Great Inagua and repairing cruise ships in Freeport. Aragonite, a type of industrial limestone, is mined from Ocean Cay's seafloor.

On a smaller scale, boat making has long been a thriving business on the Abacos. Graceful sailing vessels and rugged

Workers making clothing on Andros Island

Money Facts

The value of Bahamian dollars is equal to that of U.S. dollars, which are also accepted throughout the country. One Bahamian dollar is divided into 100 Bahamian cents. The country's bills are vibrantly colored and showcase island shells, sailboats, fish, and flowers. A portrait of Queen Elizabeth II is on the front of most of the bills, which have values of 50 cents and 1, 3, 5, 10, 20, 50, and 100 dollars.

All Bahamian coins show the national coat of arms and the date on one side. A starfish is shown on the back of the 1-cent coin, a pineapple on the 5-cent coin, a bonefish on the 10-cent coin, hibiscus flowers on the 15-cent coin, and a sailboat on the 25-cent coin.

Bahamian paper money is printed in England, and Bahamian coins are minted by the Royal Canadian Mint in Ottawa, Canada.

fishing craft are constructed under the shade of swaying palms in Man of War Cay. Many generations of skilled workers use mahogany and teak for decks and railings. Timber from the islands is used for the hulls and planking. The perfume of fresh shavings and sawdust mingle with that of flowers, making for a fragrant workspace.

Agriculture and Fishing

Over the generations, Bahamians tried growing different crops. During colonial days, cotton was a major product, but it quickly ran through the nutrients in the thin soil. In the late 1890s, tough fibrous sisal was cultivated for use as a twine used to wrap hay bales. That industry failed after production rose on a better quality Mexican fiber. In the early 2000s, a citrus disease destroyed the lime, lemon, and grapefruit industries.

Sugarcane was another crop that did not do as well as expected. A giant sugar refinery was constructed on Abaco in the 1960s. It was one of largest agricultural enterprises undertaken in the country. The effort failed because large amounts of sugar could not be produced profitably. The Bahamians were not about to give up, however. Much of the cane plantation lands were leased back to local farmers who now grow grass sod for landscapers and vegetables for markets. They also collect honey from bees.

Freshly picked bananas on Harbour Island will be shipped to other places to be sold.

Today, some two thousand people in the islands are full-time farmers. They have the advantage of a great climate but must deal with poor soil and limited water resources. On some farms, bat guano (bat droppings) is used as fertilizer. The wetter, northern islands can support large-scale commercial agriculture, while people make do with what they have in backyard gardens on the drier southern islands. About 80 percent of the farms are smaller than 10 acres (4 ha).

Neem trees are among the crops that have been successful in the Bahamas. The trees' roots, bark, leaves, seeds, flowers, and fruit are used in makeup and medicines. Potatoes, peanuts, bananas, and pineapples also grow well there.

Bahamians are working to develop thriving shrimping and fish farming industries. Brazil and China are among the country's biggest competitors in these fields.

Today, almost nine thousand fishers are active in the Bahamas. They seek out crayfish, lobster, queen conch, snapper, triggerfish, and other species in the clear, shallow waters.

Resources

Cropland	Grassland	Ls Limestone
Forests	Nonagricultural land	Na Salt
	Oil	

Conch are a common catch in the Bahamas.

An Agricultural Manufactories Act provides help to agricultural businesses. It offers them interest-free loans to purchase supplies and limits taxes on many products. Although Bahamians are trying to increase food production, they still need to import more than $250 million of food each year, about 80 percent of the food they need.

What the Bahamas Grows, Makes, and Mines

Agriculture (2008)

Chickens	3,000,000 birds
Vegetables	20,500 metric tons
Pineapples	13,000 metric tons

Manufacturing (value of exports, 2007)

Plastics	$142,200,000
Chemicals	$84,562,000
Rum	$20,282,000

Mining (2007)

Salt	882,300 metric tons
Aragonite	1,100 metric tons

Exports

The Bahamas is involved in the global business scene. The country exports about $334 million of products every year. Leading exports include mineral products, salt, rum, animal products, chemicals, fruits, and vegetables. Its primary trade partners are the United States, Canada, the Netherlands, and France. Bahamian trade representatives actively seek economic links from around the world that can be explored and nurtured. The country imports $2.6 billion worth in food products, machinery, transport equipment, manufactured goods, chemicals, and fuels. Most of the imports come from the United States and Puerto Rico.

A Mix of People

THE POPULATION OF THE BAHAMAS IS RELATIVELY young. The average age is 28.7 years, and about 30 percent of the population is between two and fourteen years old. On average, Bahamian women have two children, a rate that keeps the population stable. But in recent years, the Bahamian population has grown through immigration. Many people have moved to the islands from the United States, and many more have come from other Caribbean nations, particularly the troubled nation of Haiti.

About two-thirds of Bahamians live in the capital city of Nassau. The rest are spread in small settlements across the islands. Most villages are located in places where there is a natural harbor, which makes fishing and travel easier.

Opposite: **A mother and daughter in the Bahamas. Bahamians live an average of seventy-one years.**

Who Are the Bahamians?

Bahamians of African descent, or African Bahamians, make up 85 percent of the national population of 353,658. Most African Bahamians trace their ancestry back to West Africa. Bahamians

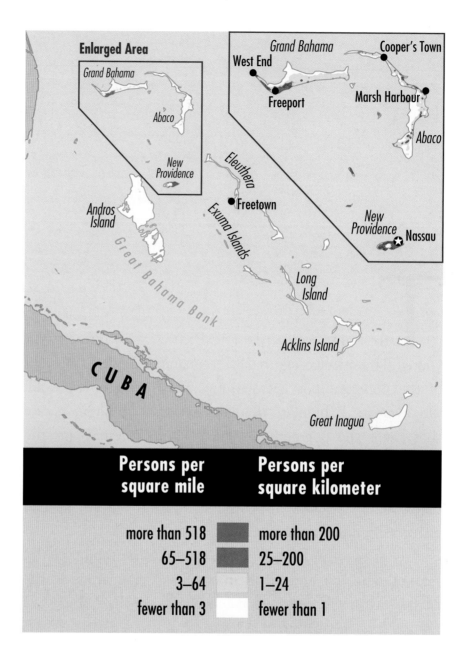

Persons per square mile

more than 518	
65–518	
3–64	
fewer than 3	

Persons per square kilometer

more than 200	
25–200	
1–24	
fewer than 1	

with European backgrounds make up about 12 percent of the population. Another 3 percent is of Asian and Hispanic heritage. Most Bahamians are actually a mix of backgrounds because of intermarriage.

The History of a Name

Many black Bahamians share the last name Rolle. This name can be traced back to Lord John Rolle, a Loyalist governor of the Bahamas. It was common for freed slaves to take the last name of their former owners. Rolle owned more than three hundred enslaved workers and vast amounts of land. Upon his death, Rolle freed all the enslaved people who worked for him and gave them his lands.

Black Bahamians

The earliest free blacks to arrive in the Bahamas came from Bermuda in the mid-1600s. Many were farmers and skilled craftspeople seeking a better way of life. Most settled on the north end of Eleuthera. Like their white neighbors, they struggled with poor soil and lack of supplies. They were also constantly afraid of being attacked by the Spanish and sold into slavery if the Spanish captured them.

Before and during the American Revolution, individuals loyal to England, or Loyalists, fled from the southern colonies, bringing their slaves with them. This influx of Loyalists shifted the racial makeup of the islands from largely white to primarily black.

By the early 1800s, many Europeans realized the evils of slavery. This trade in humans was outlawed in Britain in 1807, and the Royal Navy was ordered to commandeer ships carrying captives. If a slave ship was wrecked on a reef off the Bahamas, survivors were often given their freedom. In 1831, Bahamas governor Sir James Carmichael Smyth created villages where such survivors could start new lives. One of these communities was Adelaide, a village on the southwestern coast of New Providence. Named after the wife of King William IV of

Population of Largest Cities (2012 est.):

City	Population
Nassau, New Providence	255,789
Freeport, Grand Bahama	45,945
West End, Grand Bahama	13,577
Cooper's Town, Abaco	9,948
Marsh Harbour, Abaco	6,283

Freedom's Heritage

Gambier, a village located 9 miles (15 km) west of Nassau, was established by freed Africans after the abolition of the slave trade in the British Empire in 1807. One person who settled in Gambier was Elijah Morris, who led one of the largest slave revolts in U.S. history. In 1841, 135 Africans were being trans- ported by a ship called the *Creole*, from Virginia to New Orleans, Louisiana, where they would be sold. Under Morris's leadership, the Africans took control of the ship and headed to Nassau. Everyone on board was eventually freed. Morris's descendants still live in Gambier today.

The Albert Lowe Museum is located in a historic house in New Plymouth. The museum is dedicated to preserving the history of New Plymouth dating back to its Loyalist days.

England, Adelaide is now popular for its pristine beaches and offshore fishing.

White Bahamians

The white Loyalists who settled in the Bahamas were not accepted initially by the "old inhabitants," the islands' early white residents. The newcomers, in turn, derided these longtime settlers as "Conchy Joes," after the pink and white mollusk. Yet, in time, this division healed. Today, white Bahamians are scattered across the islands. Some live in homes much like those their ancestors lived in on the mainland of North America. Many houses in Abaco's New Plymouth look like those in New England, spruced up with brightly painted shutters.

Most white people in the Bahamas today have a British background. One percent of the Bahamian population is descended from Greek laborers who helped develop the sponging industry in the late 1880s. Many of those laborers' great-grandchildren are now lawyers, doctors, and teachers.

Ethnicity in the Bahamas

Black	85%
White	12%
Asian and Hispanic	3%

More Recent Arrivals

For generations, people of Asian descent, particularly Chinese, have lived in the Bahamas, many operating restaurants and other highly successful companies. A large number fled China

A Bahamian of Chinese descent prepares for a Junkanoo parade.

A Haitian woman gets her hair braided in Nassau. Between thirty thousand and sixty thousand Haitians live in the Bahamas.

because Communists gained control of their country after World War II. Today, with growing Chinese investment in the Bahamas, business leaders and politicians from the two countries work together closely. Thousands of Chinese construction workers have helped build major structures.

A large number of people in the Bahamas are originally from the nearby nation of Haiti. It is estimated that Haitians account for 20 to 25 percent of the population of the Bahamas. They left their impoverished home country because they could not make a living there. Haitians often do unskilled work and are sometimes looked down on by local Bahamians. The Haitians are also set apart because they speak French Creole rather than English as a first language.

Bahamian culture is a mixture of heritages, and storytelling helps keep rich traditions alive. Black Bahamians sometimes tell slightly different versions of the same stories told by white Bahamians. There are two legends about Pretty Molly, who supposedly haunts Little Exuma Island. In one story, the beautiful girl is a drowned slave whose ghost roams the beaches at night. In the other, she is a young white woman turned into a lovely mermaid. Children from many different backgrounds love the lively chronicles of rascally B'Rabby and his silly friend B'Booky. Many of these stories have lessons at their heart. The stories help children learn problem solving and the importance of taking responsibility for their actions.

Television has had a strong impact on Bahamian life, just as it has everywhere. But storytelling remains a vital art form in the nation. In recent years, the Bahamas has seen a revival in storytelling led by writers such as Patricia Glinton-Meicholas, Eloise Greenfield, and Susan J. Wallace. The

Lively Legends

Some Bahamians believe in mysterious creatures, or at least tell stories about them. When the full moon shines its brightest, Bahamians say you can hear the chick-charnies scamper through the shadows on Andros. These are red-eyed, three-fingered, three-toed elves who are usually up to no good, especially if they catch naughty children playing outside when they shouldn't be. It is said that the chickcharnies hang upside down from trees. Polite youngsters who mind their parents chase away these mischievous creatures by swatting a branch at them.

"Devil trees" are found on the windswept south shore of San Salvador. Don't steal any coconuts from these trees. Supposedly, terrible things will happen if you do. According to legend, long ago, a landowner built a high fence around his coconut grove to keep children from stealing the fruit. He also had a sorcerer cast a spell to punish those who stole his coconuts.

Words from the Past

Some words that are now part of English can be traced back to the Lucayan people of the Bahamas. Words such as *hammock* evolved from their word *hamaca*. The word *hurricane* comes from *Huracán*, the god of storms.

Commonwealth Writers of the Bahamas hosts a Story Tellers Convention every year. It even has a junior division where kids can tell stories.

Bahamian girls share some laughs.

Speaking Bahamian

English is the official language in the Bahamas. A large number of both black and white Bahamians use a dialect, or slightly different version of the language, when they speak. The rhythm and slang varies from island to island. Sometimes when speaking, people change the names of their towns. People from Flamingo Cay in the Exumas might call it Fillimingo, but everyone knows what they're talking about.

The Bahamian dialect tends to be more common on the islands that were among the first settled. Researchers say there is a significant link to the Gullah language spoken by some African Americans who live in the Sea Islands off South Carolina. The speech is similar because many Bahamians descended from enslaved people brought to the Bahamas from that region. Traces of Gaelic, the language of Ireland and Scotland, are also apparent in the Bahamian dialect if one listens carefully.

Let's Talk

Slang peppers conversation in the Bahamas. Here are a few common terms:

jack	friend
argie	argue
a leg short	being late
tote news	gossip
yinna	you all
we ga link	I'll see you later

Spiritual Life

Most Bahamians are religious. Families and friends gather for prayer, song, and conversation in churches, synagogues, and mosques. Marriages, baptisms, and funerals are important occasions.

Today, the largest religious group in the Bahamas is the Baptists. About 35 percent of Bahamians belong to the Baptist denomination, or version, of Protestantism. The next largest group is Anglican, also known as Episcopalian. They make up about 15 percent of the population. Roman Catholics account for around 13 percent of the population. Other versions of Christianity found in the Bahamas include Pentecostal, Church of God, Seventh-Day Adventist, and Methodist. Other faiths represented in the Bahamas include Judaism, Islam, Bahaism, Hindusim, and Rastafarianism.

Opposite: **A minister preaches in Nassau. More than half of Bahamians attend church at least once a month.**

Religion in the Bahamas

Baptist	35.4%
Anglican	15.1%
Roman Catholic	13.5%
Pentecostal	8.1%
Church of God	4.8%
Methodist	4.2%
Other Christian	15.2%
None or unknown	2.9%
Non-Christian	0.8%

Christianity

Christian services in the Bahamas are similar to those found in the United States and Canada. Ministers give sermons, and people read from the Bible. Music is a part of many Christian services. Some churches feature hymns played on organs. Some include bands with guitars and drums. And some services are enlivened with soulful gospel music.

Priests enter St. Andrews Anglican Church, a historic church in George Town on Great Exuma.

Upbeat Church Music

Adrian Edgecombe leads one of the most popular church choirs in the Bahamas. First known as Adrian Edgecombe & the Bahamas Harvest Church Choir and later as Adrian Edgecombe & Harvest Generation, the group mixes reggae, calypso, traditional Bahamian music called junkanoo, rhythm and blues, and hip-hop. Their albums include *Rejoice!* and *Overcomer.* By 2011, the group included thirty-two gospel singers and musicians.

Intricate handclapping sometimes helps keep the tempo for church music. In the early 1950s, musician Edmund Moxey transcribed traditional clapping patterns. The rhythms he jotted down date back to the days of slavery.

Singing is central to many church services in the Bahamas.

Stone by Stone

Father Jerome (1876–1956), whose real name was John C. Hawes, was a priest and a trained architect born in England. He designed and built many churches in the Bahamas. He built a chapel on Cat Island at the top of a steep hill that he renamed Mount Alvernia. The stones he used for construction he carried up the slope by hand. At this site, he could pray in peace, soothed by looking out at the wide sea. This stone chapel, called the Hermitage, still stands today.

On the islands there is a special devotion to Mary, the mother of Jesus, and several churches carry her name. The original St. Mary's Anglican Church on Virginia Street in Nassau was destroyed by a hurricane in 1866. It was quickly rebuilt and remains a center of community life.

Nassau's St. Matthew's Church is the oldest standing church on the islands. Initially, Nassau's church was a small wooden room built in the 1700s. A rugged stone structure that became St. Matthew's followed. It has a towering steeple and thick walls. The initial services in the new building were held in 1802. For many years, the clock in the steeple was considered one of the only reliable timepieces on New Providence. Richardson Saunders became the church's priest in 1856. He was the first Episcopal priest ordained in the Bahamas.

Obeah

Some people in the Bahamas practice Obeah. This folk religion is practiced throughout the Caribbean and Brazil. It mixes some European traditions with African beliefs, mostly from the Igbo people of West Africa. In Obeah, charms are used for magical purposes. It is thought that these charms can bring good or bad fortune, even a win in a ball game or success in business. Obeah can also make the rich poor if they are greedy and take advantage of other people.

During colonial days, Obeah practitioners were regularly put to death as witches. Historians say that Obeah was one way that enslaved people could secretly rebel against their masters.

St. John's Anglican Church is the oldest church on Harbour Island. It dates back to 1768.

People at Vodou ceremonies usually wear white as a sign of purity.

Vodou

Vodou is another mixture of African traditions and Christianity. This religion is common in Haiti, and the Haitians who have moved to the Bahamas in recent years have brought it to their new home. The word *Vodou* is of Dahomean origin. Dahomey was a kingdom in coastal West Africa, once the center of the slave trade.

Spirits called *lwas* are at the center of the Vodou faith. These spirits can communicate with humans. There are many different lwas in Vodou, and each has its own personality. To communicate with the lwas, people practicing Vodou perform different songs and dances. Vodou ceremonies are held to communicate with lwas and dead relatives. During these ceremonies, people sometimes go into trances while singing and dancing.

Folk Medicine

Bahamian folk medicine has a lot of healing power. More than one hundred plants in the islands have been used to cure a variety of illnesses. Bark from the gumbo-limbo tree is commonly used to treat skin sores, measles, and sunburn. Potted basil, which Bahamians call basily, is helpful in treating asthma and chest colds. These treatments have been used for hundreds of years, but now they are becoming less common. Folk medicine is slowly fading away as modern medical practices become more prevalent and elderly Bahamians die off, taking their knowledge of plants, roots, and leaves with them.

The bark of the gumbo-limbo tree is thin, red, and peeling.

CHAPTER NINE

Island Art

BAHAMIANS LIKE TO HAVE FUN. SINGING, ART, dancing, and sports are all popular. It's even better when all these activities can be put together in one package, as they are in Exuma's annual Bahamian Music and Heritage Festival. The event features a boating regatta; cooking demonstrations; art exhibits; and foot-tapping, get-up-and-dance music. There are also other music festivals for all tastes, ranging from the Bahamas Jazz Rhythm and Blues Festival to the annual Freetown Cha Cha Festival.

Opposite: **Musicians perform on Cat Island.**

Making Music

Bahamians readily admit to their love of music. They are eager to listen, applaud, sing, and dance to a smooth heel-and-toe polka, a jump dance, or a graceful quadrille. Most of the music is lively, whether in a nightclub or in a church sanctuary. Crowds turn out to hear the Royal Bahamas Police Force Band perform at public events and fill concert halls. The Nassau

Music Society organizes and promotes musical concerts and activities throughout the Bahamas.

A music form particular to the Bahamas is junkanoo. Bugles and drums are at the center of this type of music. Bahamians are happy to put their own twist on the best music from other countries. A style called rake and scrape evolved from the musical traditions of the Turks and Caicos Islands.

A young Bahamian plays the saw by bending it and scraping its edge with a nail.

The Baha Men perform at a festival in Florida.

Musicians use a carpenter's saw as an instrument, scraping the jagged blade with a nail. Drums, guitars, accordions, and other instruments accompany the saw.

Lively calypso music is also common in the Bahamas, where it is called goombay. It originated in Trinidad and Tobago and then spread throughout the Caribbean. It evolved into its own Bahamian version. Pianist George Symonette was hugely popular in the 1930s and 1940s and is often called the Father of Bahamian Calypso.

Noted island musicians are recognized around the world for their talents. The Baha Men play a modern version of junkanoo music. Their song "Who Let the Dogs Out" was a huge hit around the world and is often played at sporting events.

The Godfather Sings

Ronnie Butler is a Bahamian calypso and rake and scrape entertainer who is called the Godfather of Bahamian Music. Born in 1937 on New Providence, Butler began his professional performing career at the age of sixteen while working in construction. As a teen, he worked all day on a job site and then went to his late-night music gig at a Nassau hotel.

Eventually becoming a noted nightclub and concert guitarist, Butler toured Europe and South and North America. His hits include "Burma Road," "Going Back to the Island," and "Pretty Brown Eyes." During his career, he recorded more than fifteen albums and won dozens of international awards. Queen Elizabeth II knighted him for his accomplishments.

The National Art Gallery of the Bahamas focuses on the work of Bahamian artists.

Orlando Francis, who works under the name Landlord, is a renowned gospel reggae artist from Nassau. His 2004 album "We Need Peace" is a gospel classic.

NATIONAL ART GALLERY OF THE BAHAMAS

Stan Burnside's work features strong figures and vibrant colors.

Always There Is Art

Many different Bahamian artists have made their mark both locally and globally. The Bahamas scenery and its people are the favorite subjects of printmaker Maxwell Taylor and painter Stan Burnside. They are true locals with a keen eye for the swirl of island life. When self-taught painter Amos Ferguson of Exuma died in 2009, at age eighty-nine, the nation mourned the loss of one of its artistic greats. His works have been shown around the world and are noted for their lively themes and bold colors. Antonius Roberts is a sculptor and conservationist who focuses on nature and spirituality.

In 1984, Nassau native Sonia Isaacs was the first Bahamian female painter to have a major one-woman show in the United States. She also makes pottery, which is prized for its texture and graceful designs. Photographer Sacha-Kathleen Hadland magnificently blends light and shadows to capture the beauty of the island people she portrays.

In 2011, the Bahamas' Public Treasury Department turned the first five floors of its Nassau office into an art gallery featuring the works of the Bahamas' top female artists. The extensive display, entitled *Bahama Mama*, featured young artists such as crochet designer Leah Eneas, high fashion designer Apryl Burrows, and Mardia Powell, whose works are constructed with delightful fabrics.

Chantal E. Y. Bethel is an artist who was born in Haiti and now lives in the Bahamas. Much of her work focuses on the lives of Caribbean women.

The novels of Wendy Coakley-Thompson explore race relations.

A World of Words

Bahamian authors have placed a permanent mark on the literary world. Some of the most recognized writers are women. In her Bahamian patois, or dialect, folklorist and poet Susan J. Wallace once wrote, "Somebody bes' start writin'/Somebody bes write fas'/'Cause it done too late already/Ta keep up wid de pas'." Readers love Wallace's beautifully crisp use of words, which is often studied in Bahamian schools.

Wendy Coakley-Thompson is the author of the popular novels *Back to Life* and *What You Won't Do for Love*. She was raised in Nassau and, although she now lives in the United

Spooky Business

Alphonso Smith did not begin his career intending to be a writer. Instead, he was a policeman and the assistant director of immigration in the Bahamas. But later in life, he wrote many children's stories based on his own experiences growing up in the small settlement of Victoria Point on Andros. Children today still get the shivers when reading "The Ghost of Hog Head Grape Tree" and "Ghost in the Church."

States, she still writes for Bahamian publications and is a National Public Radio commentator. Many of her works deal with relationships between blacks and whites. Bahamian poets Patrick Rahming, Robert Johnson, and Obediah Smith produce finely crafted works that sizzle with life.

Obediah Smith is the author of seventeen books of poetry.

Ian Strachan has made his mark writing plays. *God's Angry Babies* is a hard-hitting play depicting a young Bahamian man struggling on his way to adulthood. Besides writing plays, Strachan teaches English at the College of the Bahamas.

The Bahamas prizes its writers as national treasures and nurtures them in their careers. Authors flock to the intensive Bahamas Writers Summer Institute held each year on the campus of the College of the Bahamas in Nassau. This creative writing program unites beginning and experienced writers in exploring their craft.

The Bahamas' easy lifestyle has attracted writers from other parts of the world. They come to the Bahamas seeking ideas and relaxation. American novelist Ernest Hemingway often visited

Busy Man

An actor, playwright, director, producer, and lawyer, Winston Saunders (1941–2006) did it all. Throughout his life, he kept creatively busy. Saunders was the author of two prominent Bahamian plays, *Them* and *You Can Lead a Horse to Water*. He and Philip Burrows cowrote the libretto of *Our Boys*, the first Bahamian opera, and codirected the production as well. He was chairman of the Dundas Centre for the Performing Arts from 1975 to 1998, where he mentored young Bahamian writers and actors. Saunders also founded the National Youth Choir, the National Children's Choir, and the National Dance Company. At the time of his death, he was chairman of the Bahamas' National Commission on Cultural Development and planning the commemoration of the two hundredth anniversary of the abolition of the slave trade in the British Empire.

Bimini, staying at the Compleat Angler Hotel. He loved sport-fishing and once caught an Atlantic blue marlin that weighed 500 pounds (230 kg). This feat was said to have inspired him to write his famous novel *The Old Man and the Sea*. In the Bahamas, Hemingway also finished his novel *To Have and Have Not* and several magazine stories. When he died in 1961, he was working on *Islands in the Stream*, a tale involving deep-sea fishing off Alice Town on North Bimini.

At the Movies

Sidney Poitier is the most famous actor of Bahamian heritage. Poitier's family hailed from Cat Island, but he was born pre-

Ernest Hemingway posing with a huge tuna. Hemingway lived on Bimini from 1935 to 1937.

U.S. president Barack Obama awarded Sidney Poitier the Presidential Medal of Freedom in 2009. The Medal of Freedom is the highest nonmilitary honor in the United States.

maturely in Miami, Florida, where his parents had gone to sell vegetables from their farm. He grew up on Cat Island and in Nassau before moving to Miami at age fifteen. Within a few years, he moved to New York, joined the army, and studied acting at the American Negro Theater. He went on to stage success and then began making movies. In 1958, for his work in *The Defiant Ones*, he became the first black male actor to be nominated for an Academy Award. In 1963, he won an Oscar for *Lilies of the Field*, becoming the first black man to win the Academy Award for Best Actor. Poitier has received many career awards. In 1999, the American Film Institute included him in their list of the top twenty-five greatest male stars of all time.

Poitier was a strong supporter of the civil rights movement, and in 2009, President Barack Obama awarded him the Presidential Medal of Freedom.

Another notable Bahamian actor is Persia White. She was born in Miami in 1972 but grew up in the Bahamas. She has performed in many films and on television shows. One of her best roles was in the long-running television program, *Girlfriends*. White is also a singer. In 2009, she released her debut album, *Mecca*.

Persia White has appeared on many television shows, including *Girlfriends*, *Angel*, and *The Vampire Diaries*.

The Bahamas has provided fabulous landscapes for dozens of films. Directors love the great weather, the clear skies, and brilliant blue water. The Bahamas Film and Television Commission helps directors find the perfect locales for their films. English author Ian Fleming used to vacation in the Bahamas and used the islands as the setting in several of his James Bond spy thrillers. Paradise Island, Inagua, and Nassau were perfect places for the action-packed movies based on the novels.

Filmmakers have been shooting movies in the Bahamas for decades. The Walt Disney Company filmed parts of the 1954 movie *20,000 Leagues Under the Sea* there.

Many James Bond movies have been filmed in the Bahamas. In 1981, Roger Moore played the spy in *For Your Eyes Only*.

In addition to providing the backdrop for films, Bahamians are also involved in the making of movies. Underwater cameraman and stuntman Gavin McKinney doubled for both Sean Connery and Pierce Brosnan, actors who portrayed the master spy 007 in several Bond movies. The 2009 Bahamas

International Film Festival (BIFF) honored McKinney with the first Bahamian Tribute Award for his photographic and acting achievements.

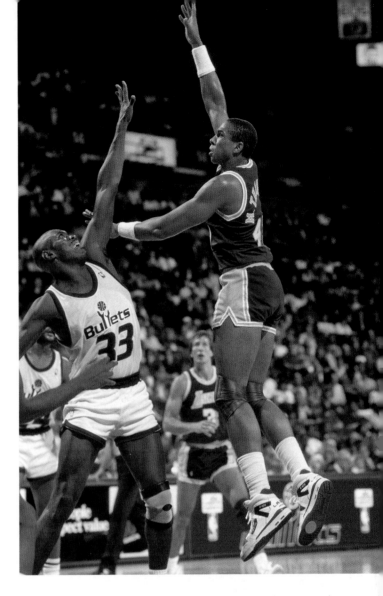

Pushing the Body

When kids play basketball, they might pretend they are Mychal Thompson, a Bahamian who played for the Los Angeles Lakers and other teams in the United States. After years of bouncing and shooting a ball, Thompson moved over to the radio booth to become a sports commentator.

Rick Fox also played for the Lakers, as well as the Boston Celtics. Although born in Toronto, Canada, he grew up in the Bahamas where he attended Kingsway Academy in Nassau. After his basketball career ended, Fox appeared in several movies and TV shows.

Bahamians compete in sports events around the world wearing the national colors of aquamarine, gold, and black. Cara Veron Saunders of Freeport is a sprint and long jump athlete. At the 2001 Junior Olympics, she won a gold medal in both the 100-meter race and the long jump, and a silver medal in the 100-meter relay.

Mychal Thompson (jumping, in blue) was the first choice in the 1978 National Basketball Association draft, when professional teams take turns choosing college players. It was the first time a foreign-born player had ever been the top pick.

Talented Sports Family

Nassau's Tonique Williams-Darling (center) is a sprinter who won a gold medal in the 400-meter race at the 2004 Summer Olympics in Greece. She has also captured medals in many other international competitions. For her accomplishments, the government named a major road on New Providence in her honor, calling it the Tonique Williams-Darling Highway. She is married to Dennis Darling, another Nassau-born track star, who now coaches at Texas Christian University in Fort Worth, Texas.

Dennis is the older brother of Devard Darling, one of the first Bahamians to play in the National Football League. He is a wide receiver who signed with the Houston Texans in 2011 after several years playing with the Kansas City Chiefs and Baltimore Ravens.

Devard shared his football playing dreams with his twin brother, Devaughn, who died during a football practice at Florida State University in 2001. In his brother's honor, Devard set up the As One Foundation to help young Bahamians learn about American football. Aided by his cousin Frank Rutherford, Devard also established summer football camps in the Bahamas.

Rutherford, another great athlete from the Bahamas, competed in three Olympics. In 1992, he won a bronze medal in the triple jump. With that victory, he became the first Bahamian track-and-field Olympic medalist.

Bahamians have also excelled at tennis. Freeport's Roger Smith and Nassau's Mark Knowles have done well at the Olympics and playing the professional circuit. Another top-ranked player from the Bahamas, Devin Mullings, played men's singles at the 2008 Olympic Games and is now playing professionally.

Mark Knowles has won more than fifty doubles titles in his career.

Daily Doings

LIFE IN THE BAHAMAS OFTEN SEEMS RELAXED. PEOPLE lie on the beautiful beaches and wiggle their toes in the warm, white sand. They go for a dip in the striking blue water. Or maybe they just lounge under the breeze-touched shade of a palm tree, sipping a Bahamas Goombay Punch soda, with its snappy pineapple flavor and touch of lemon.

But life in the Bahamas isn't all a vacation. Children go to school. Parents cook dinner. People go to work. Life goes on.

School Days

Education takes up a large part of the government's budget. About 24 percent of the national budget goes toward education. There are 210 primary and secondary schools in the Bahamas. About three-quarters of these schools are operated by the government, and one-quarter is independently or privately managed. No tuition is required at government schools. The Bahamas Ministry of Education monitors schools and their performance. Among the top private schools are

Opposite: **A dip in the sea is an everyday part of life in the Bahamas.**

All schools in the Bahamas, both public and private, require students to wear uniforms.

St. Andrews, Lyford Cay, Tambearly, and Kingsway Academy. Each school has its own school uniform that the students wear, so it is easy to tell which school a child attends.

In the Bahamas, 95 percent of adults can read and write, and good scholars are highly respected. Many students study French and Spanish. They know those languages will help them land a job with an international firm, which allows them to travel overseas. Mandarin Chinese is becoming a more popu-

Young Spelling Champ

Spelling *obelisk* correctly earned nine-year-old Yelena Persaud a victory at the thirteenth annual Bahamas National Spelling Bee in 2010. (An obelisk is a tall stone pillar that serves as a landmark.) The sixth grader at St. Francis de Sales Catholic School in Marsh Harbour, Abaco, topped nineteen other students to walk away with the first prize. This made her the youngest contestant ever to capture the crown. Yelena then went on to be among the top fifty spellers at the Scripps National Spelling Bee in Washington, D.C.

lar language to learn in upper grades because of the growing commercial links between the Bahamas and China.

Children in the Bahamas are required to go to school from ages five to sixteen.

Schools follow the British form of education, where first- to sixth-grade students advance depending on their exam performance each year. In secondary school, pupils take the National Junior Certificate Examination and must pass tests in order to graduate. From there, they can go on to the College of the Bahamas, the Princess Margaret Hospital School of Nursing, the Bahamas Technical and Vocational Institute, or the University of the West Indies Centre for Hotel and Tourism Management. When they get scholarships, many students travel to Canada, Britain, or the United States for their university studies.

Ringing Around

Ring play is a favorite children's game in the Bahamas and nearby island countries. Players get into a big circle and hold hands. One person jumps into the middle and dances while everyone else sings "show me your motion." Then the person in the middle picks somebody else and that child moves into the center of the ring. There are many songs that go with ring play, such as the traditional "Brown Girl in the Ring."

Brown girl in the ring
Tra la la la la
There's a brown girl in the ring
Tra la la la la la
Brown girl in the ring
Tra la la la la
She looks like a sugar in a plum
Plum plum

Show me your motion
Tra la la la la
Come on show me your motion
Tra la la la la la
Show me your motion
Tra la la la la
She looks like a sugar in a plum
Plum plum

Skip across the ocean
Tra la la la la
Come on skip across the ocean
Tra la la la la la
Skip across the ocean
Tra la la la la
She looks like a sugar in a plum
Plum plum.

National Holidays

New Year's Day	January 1
Good Friday	March or April
Easter	March or April
Whit Monday	May or June
Labor Day	June
Independence Day	July 10
Emancipation Day	August
Discovery Day	October 12
Christmas Day	December 25
Boxing Day	December 26

Housing

There are few tall buildings in the Bahamas. In part, that is because they are less sturdy in hurricanes. Most buildings are made of either limestone or wood. The years have not been kind to many old colonial buildings. The heavy wind and rain are hard on the wooden structures, causing them to erode and decay. And many wooden buildings have also been damaged by termites. Because of such threats, cement buildings are common today.

Some Bahamians live in grand houses. Others live in run-down shacks. Whenever possible, houses have porches and lots of windows, so the warm breezes can pass through.

Good Food

All kinds of food can be found in the Bahamas. People enjoy Chinese food and Thai food, hamburgers and pizza. More typical Bahamian cooking often uses fish and seafood. Fish and chips are common, as are chowders. Conch is a favorite

Keep Left

Visitors from North America have to be extra careful when driving in the Bahamas. Because it was once a British colony, the Bahamas follows the British way of driving, which is on the left side of the road. Americans and Canadians have to remind themselves not to drive on the right, like they do in their home countries.

food to use in chowder. It is also frequently made into fritters or added to salads.

For breakfast, Bahamians often eat fresh fruit along with white grits (cornmeal) made into porridge. Souse (pronounced

An old building in Nassau

Conch fritters are a popular food in the Bahamas. They are by made by frying chopped conch meat that has been mixed with onion, celery, garlic, eggs, and other ingredients.

SUSE) is a traditional soup, often made with onions, lime juice, celery, peppers, and meat such as chicken or lamb tongue. Some people eat souse accompanied by a huge slice of warm johnny-cake, which is a kind of corn bread. Rice and peas, potato salad, and macaroni and cheese are also popular dishes.

Guava duff is a common dessert. To make guava duff, Bahamians boil guava fruit rolled in dough and then cover the mixture with a butter sauce.

Nassau Neighborhoods

Many neighborhoods in Nassau have a strong history and atmosphere all their own. Many Yoruba people from what is now Nigeria in western Africa lived in Nango Town after liberation. Congo Town, meanwhile, was home to freed slaves with Central African roots. Burnside Town was populated by Bahamian-born Creoles of black and mixed race. If a guide says an area is "over the hill," that literally means over the East Street hill that runs near downtown Bay Street. This neighborhood is marked by narrow streets and faded, old houses. Lyford Cay, on the western tip of New Providence, is the home of many people among the country's business and political elite. Here, lovely colonial-era mansions face the cool blue waters of Montagu Bay.

Fun in the Sun

In the Bahamas, people love to get outside and enjoy themselves. Sports are very popular. Many people play soccer, which Bahamians call football, and cricket, which is somewhat similar to baseball. Both soccer and cricket were

Like baseball, cricket is played with a ball and bat. It is popular around the world in places that were once part of the British Empire.

Bahamian Macaroni and Cheese

Bahamians love macaroni and cheese. They often add a splash of hot sauce to spice up the flavor. Have an adult help you with this recipe.

Ingredients

8 ounces macaroni

1 tablespoon finely chopped onion

1 tablespoon finely chopped green pepper

1 tablespoon finely chopped celery

6 ounces cheddar cheese, grated

Salt and pepper to taste

1 tablespoon evaporated milk

Hot sauce (optional)

Directions

Cook macaroni according to directions on the box. Preheat oven to 350°F. In a pot, combine the cooked macaroni with the onion, green pepper, and celery. Stir.

Add half of the cheese and stir over low heat until melted. Add salt and pepper and then add the evaporated milk.

Spoon into a greased 8 x 8 inch baking pan, and sprinkle the remaining cheese over the top. Bake for 20 minutes. Let cool for 10 minutes, and then cut into squares to serve. Add hot sauce if you dare. Enjoy!

Seashore Treasures

Collecting seashells is a popular pastime in the Bahamas. About a thousand varieties of seashells can be found along Bahamian beaches, particularly on Abaco and in the waters of Exuma Sound. One of the greatest prizes is the conch shell. Conchs are large mollusks that live along coral reefs or in sea grass beds. Conchs are a favorite of Bahamian cooks. Their pink meat is rich in protein and is often used in stews, fritters, or chowders. The large conch shells typically have a spiral point on one end. The empty shells are used for everything from musical instruments to garden decorations.

brought to the Bahamas by the British. In recent years, many young Bahamians have begun playing basketball.

Although the Bahamas is an island country, fishing there is not as easy as stepping out the front door and dropping a line into the ocean. It takes skill, patience, and luck to reel in "the big one." The Bahamas Wahoo Championships and Bacardi Rum Billfish Tournament draw competitors eager to land a trophy. A glass-bottom boat helps fishers see the fish scooting around in the water. Pieces of conch or crabmeat make the best bait. Fishers toss a weighted line into the sea and wait for a nibble. A slow tug probably means a grouper or snapper is sampling the goodies, while fast picks indicate a smaller triggerfish. Hungry barracuda can swiftly snatch up a catch if it isn't taken aboard quickly enough.

Deep-sea fishing requires an experienced guide and qualified boat captain. Their help is needed when battling a huge

Three Sports in One

Imagine swimming in the ocean, cycling through busy city streets, and running along a sandy beach, one right after another. That's what competitors do in the Conchman Triathlon, a major sporting contest that draws local and international triathletes to Taino Beach in Freeport. Even hardy children as young as six years old can compete, though on a smaller course.

shark, marlin, or swordfish. Plenty of photos are snapped dockside when a prize fish is strung up and weighed.

People in the Bahamas also enjoy exploring underwater while scuba diving or snorkeling. People who like lots of action can often be found waterskiing, windsurfing, and para-sailing. There are plenty activities for everyone.

Windsurfing is a mix of sailing and surfing. It is popular throughout the Bahamas.

Timeline

Bahamian History

The Lucayan people arrive in the Inaguas.   500–800 CE

Christopher Columbus lands at San   1492
Salvador and claims the
islands for Spain.

The Eleutherian Adventurers establish   1648
a colony in Governor's Harbour.

English settlers establish a community   1656
on New Providence.

Wealthy businessmen are granted   1670
approval to colonize the Bahamas.

The Spanish destroy Charles Town.   1684

The pirate Blackbeard makes Nassau   1715
his headquarters.

Woodes Rogers becomes royal   1718
governor and crushes the pirate trade.

World History

ca. 2500 BCE   The Egyptians build the pyramids
and the Sphinx in Giza.

ca. 563 BCE   The Buddha is born in India.

313 CE   The Roman emperor Constantine
legalizes Christianity.

610   The Prophet Muhammad begins preaching
a new religion called Islam.

1054   The Eastern (Orthodox) and Western
(Roman Catholic) Churches break apart.

1095   The Crusades begin.

1215   King John seals the Magna Carta.

1300s   The Renaissance begins in Italy.

1347   The plague sweeps through Europe.

1453   Ottoman Turks capture Constantinople,
conquering the Byzantine Empire.

1492   Columbus arrives in North America.

1500s   Reformers break away from the Catholic
Church, and Protestantism is born.

Bahamian History

The Bahamas are occupied by the Spanish.	1782
The Bahamas are returned to the British.	1783
Loyalists flee the new United States for the Bahamas.	1783–1784
The British outlaw the slave trade.	1807
The Emancipation Act forbids slavery throughout the British Empire.	1834
Freed African slaves make their home in the village of Gambier.	1841
The Bahamas becomes a haven for blockade runners to Southern ports during the American Civil War.	1861–1865
Rumrunners use the Bahamas as a base for shipping alcohol into the United States during Prohibition.	1920–1933
U.S. and British military bases are set up in the Bahamas during World War II.	1944–1945
The Hawksbill Creek Agreement is signed, establishing a duty-free zone in Freeport.	1955
The Bahamas gets a new constitution.	1964
The Bahamas achieves independence.	1973
The Bahamas lends officers to help a multinational force restore civilian rule to nearby Haiti.	1994
Hurricane Irene hammers the Bahamas.	2011

World History

1776	The U.S. Declaration of Independence is signed.
1789	The French Revolution begins.
1865	The American Civil War ends.
1879	The first practical lightbulb is invented.
1914	World War I begins.
1917	The Bolshevik Revolution brings communism to Russia.
1929	A worldwide economic depression begins.
1939	World War II begins.
1945	World War II ends.
1957	The Vietnam War begins.
1969	Humans land on the Moon.
1975	The Vietnam War ends.
1989	The Berlin Wall is torn down as communism crumbles in Eastern Europe.
1991	The Soviet Union breaks into separate states.
2001	Terrorists attack the World Trade Center in New York City and the Pentagon near Washington, D.C.
2004	A tsunami in the Indian Ocean destroys coastlines in Africa, India, and Southeast Asia.
2008	The United States elects its first African American president.

Fast Facts

Official name: Commonwealth of the Bahamas

Capital: Nassau

Official language: English

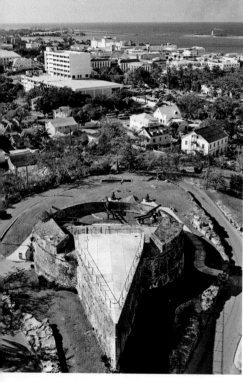

Nassau

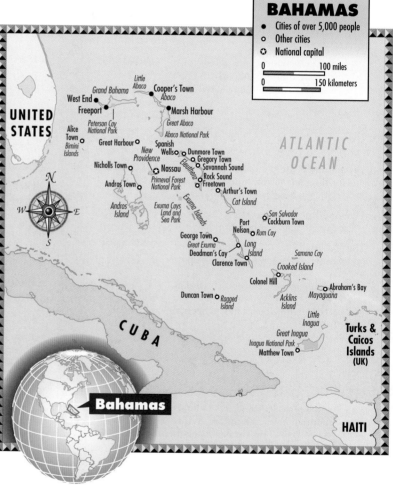

BAHAMAS
- • Cities of over 5,000 people
- ○ Other cities
- ✪ National capital

0   100 miles

0   150 kilometers

UNITED STATES

Little Abaco

Grand Bahama

Cooper's Town

West End

Freeport

Abaco

Marsh Harbour

Alice Town

Peterson Cay National Park

Great Abaco

Bimini Islands

Great Harbour

Spanish Wells

Abaco National Park

New Providence

Dunmore Town

Gregory Town

Nicholls Town

Nassau

Savannah Sound

Rock Sound

Andros Town

Primeval Forest National Park

Freetown

Arthur's Town

Cat Island

Andros Island

Exuma Cays Land and Sea Park

Eleuthera

Exuma Islands

San Salvador

Cockburn Town

Port Nelson

Rum Cay

George Town

Great Exuma

Long Island

Deadman's Cay

Clarence Town

Samana Cay

Crooked Island

Colonel Hill

Duncan Town

Ragged Island

Acklins Island

Mayaguana

Abraham's Bay

ATLANTIC OCEAN

Little Inagua

CUBA

Great Inagua

Turks & Caicos Islands (UK)

Inagua National Park

Matthew Town

HAITI

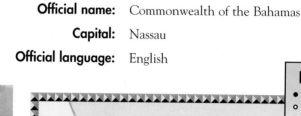

Bahamas

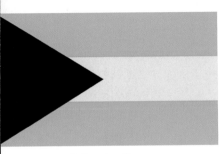

Bahamian flag

Official religion:	None
Year of founding:	1670, as a British protectorate; July 10, 1973, as Commonwealth of the Bahamas
National anthem:	"March On, Bahamaland"
Type of government:	Constitutional monarchy
Chief of state:	British monarch
Head of government:	Prime minister
Area of country:	5,382 square miles (13,939 sq km)
Latitude and longitude of Nassau:	25°5'0" N, 77°21'0" W
Closest countries:	United States, Cuba, Haiti, and the Dominican Republic
Highest elevation:	Mount Alvernia, 206 feet (63 m) above sea level
Lowest elevation:	Sea level
Average annual precipitation:	44 inches (112 cm)
National population (2010 est.):	353,658

Coral reef

Hermitage

Currency

Population of major cities (2012 est.):

Nassau, New Providence	255,789
Freeport, Grand Bahama	45,945
West End, Grand Bahama	13,577
Cooper's Town, Abaco	9,948
Marsh Harbour, Abaco	6,283

Landmarks:

▶ *Dean's Blue Hole,* Long Island

▶ *Exuma Cays Land and Sea Park*, Exuma Islands

▶ *Fort Fincastle*, Nassau

▶ *Hermitage*, Cat Island

▶ *Hope Town Lighthouse*, Great Abaco

Economy: Tourism is the most important segment of the Bahamian economy, with banking being the second. Fishing, food processing, pharmaceutical manufacturing, and salt production also play a large role in the Bahamian economy.

Currency: The Bahamian dollar. One Bahamian dollar equals one U.S. dollar, and both are accepted on the islands.

System of weights and measures: Imperial system

Literacy rate (2006): 95%

Schoolgirl

Tonique Williams-Darling

Common Bahamian words and phrases:

jack	friend
argie	argue
a leg short	being late
tote news	gossip
yinna	you all
we ga link	I'll see you later

Prominent Bahamians:

Ronnie Butler   (1937–)
Musician

Wendy Coakley-Thompson   (1966–)
Author

Lord Dunmore   (ca. 1730–1809)
Royal governor

Lynden O. Pindling   (1930–2000)
First Bahamian prime minister

Sidney Poitier   (1927–)
Actor

Winston Saunders   (1941–2006)
Playwright

Tonique Williams-Darling   (1976–)
Olympic gold medal sprinter

To Find Out More

Books

▶ Barlas, Robert, and Yong Jui Lin. *Bahamas*. New York: Marshall Cavendish Benchmark, 2011.

▶ Earle, Sylvia A. *Coral Reefs*. Washington, DC: National Geographic, 2003.

▶ Neely, Wayne. *The Great Bahamas Hurricane of 1866*. iUniverse, Inc., 2011.

▶ Turner, Telcine. *Climbing Clouds: Stories and Poems from the Bahamas*. London: Macmillan Caribbean, 1988.

Music

▶ *The Bahamas: Islands of Song*. Smithsonian Folkways, 1997.

▶ *The Real Bahamas*. Nonesuch Records, 1998.

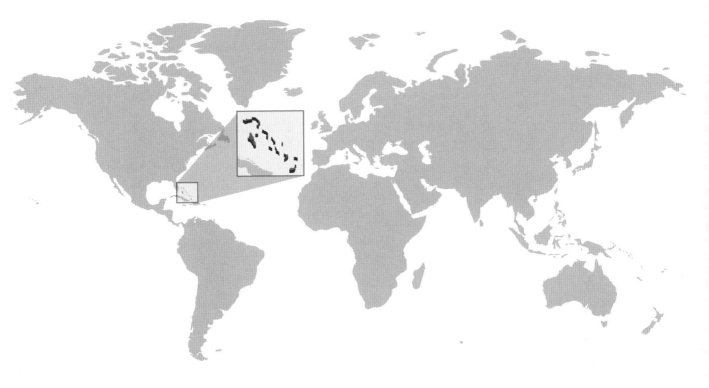

▶ Visit this Scholastic Web site for more information on the Bahamas:
www.factsfornow.scholastic.com
Enter the keyword **Bahamas**

Index

Page numbers in *italics* indicate illustrations.

A

Abaco Island, 19, 20, 21, 29, 35, 39
Abaco Wild Horse Preserve, 20
actors, 107, 108–110, *109*, *110*, 112, *112*, 133
Adelaide, 83–84
Age of Discovery, 43
agriculture
    Abaco Island, 21
    Agricultural Manufactories Act, 78
    backyard gardens, 77
    crops, 45, 52, *52*, 75–76, *76*, 77
    economy and, 55, 73, 75–77, 78, 79
    fertilizer, 77
    livestock, 26
    Lucayan people, 45
    pineapple, 21, 55, 75, 77, 79
    plantations, 52, 76
    slavery, 52–53
    soil, 77
    timber industry, 77
    topsoil, 17
airports, 57, 70
Albert Lowe Museum, 84
allamanda plants, 35
American Revolution, 51
amphibian life, 40
Andros Island, 16, 18, *22*, 23, 26, 50, *74*

animal life
    Abaco Wild Horse Preserve, 20
    Bahamian hutias, 39–40, 45
    birds, 28, 38–39, *39*
    endangered species, 41, *41*
    livestock, 26
    wild donkeys, 27, *27*
art, 103–104, *103*, *104*
As One Foundation, 114

B

Bacardi Rum Billfish Tournament, 126
Bahama Mama art display, 104
Baha Mar resort, 71
Bahamas Film and Television Commission, 111
Bahamas International Film Festival (BIFF), 112–113
Bahamas Reef Environment Educational Foundation (BREEF), 23
Bahamas Sea Turtle Conservation Group, 40
Bahamas Wahoo Championships, 126
Bahamas Writers Summer Institute, 107
Baha Men (music group), 101, *101*
Bahamian Assembly, 53
Bahamian dollar, 75, *75*
Bahamian hutias, 39–40, 41, 45
Bahamian Music and Heritage Festival, 99
barracudas, 37, *37*
Bay Street Boys, 58
Bethel, Chantal E. Y., *104*
Bimini Islands, 22
birds, 28, 38–39, *39*
Blackbeard. *See* Teach, Edward.
blockade runners, 54–55, *54*
blue holes, 26, *26*
boiling holes, 26
Bonny, Anne, 50
bottlebrush tree, 34, *34*
bougainvillea plants, 36
breadfruit trees, 33
Bruce, Peter Henry, 71

Burnside, Stan, 103, *103*
Burrows, Apryl, 104
Burrows, Philip, 107
Butler, Ronnie, 102, 133
Butler, Sir Milo B., 61–62

C

calypso music, 101
Caribbean pine trees, 18, 25, 31
Cat Island, 17, 94, 98
caves, 26, *26*, 27, 37–38
Central Andros National Park, 41
Charles I, king of England, 48
Charles, prince of Wales, 59
chickcharnies, 87
China, 71, 77, 85–86, 118–119
Christ Church Cathedral, 65
Christie, Harold, 56–57
Christie, Perry, 60, 62
cities. *See also* towns; villages.
    Cooper's Town, 21, 83
    Freeport, 15, 18, *19*, 21, *21*, 70, 74, 83, 127
    Marsh Harbour, 20, 83
    Nassau, 8, 9, 11, 15, 16, 21, 25, 33, 50, 51, *51*, *53*, 57, *57*, 59, 63, 64, 65, *65*, 68, 71, 81, 83, 86, 90, 94, 99–100, 102, 104, *122*, 124
    New Plymouth, 84, *84*
climate, 16, 17–18, 28–29, *29*, 31, 77, 94, 121
clothing, 9, 10, *10*, *13*, 28, 65, *74*, *118*
Coakley-Thompson, Wendy, 105–106, *105*, 133
coastline, 12, *14*, 16, 25, 26, 33, *33*, 76, 84, 87, 117, 126, *126*, 127
Columbus, Christopher, *42*, 43–44, *44*, 45–46
Commonwealth Writers of the Bahamas, 88
communications, 13, 87
Conchman Triathlon, 127, *127*
conchs, 36, 77, *78*, 121–122, *123*, 126
Constituencies Commission, 64

constitution, 58, 59, 61
construction industry, 69, 86
Cooper's Town, 21, 83
coral reefs, 23, *23*, 36–37, *36*, 41, 50, 126, *126*, 131
Court of Appeal, 62, 66–67, *66*
crayfish, 24, 77
crepe myrtle plant, 35, *35*
crime, 72

D

dancing, 8, 9, 10, 96, 99
Darling, Dennis, 114
Darling, Devard, 114
Darling, Devaughn, 114
Deadman's Cay, 27
Dean's Blue Hole, 26
Deveaux, Andrew, 51
"devil trees," 87
Dundas Centre for the Performing Arts, 107
Dunmore, Lord, 25, 133
Dunmore Town, 25
duty-free zone, 70

E

economy
    Agricultural Manufactories Act, 78
    agriculture and, 55, 73, 75–77, 78, 79
    Bahamian dollar, 75, *75*
    duty-free zone, 70
    exports, 78–79
    fishing industry, 22, 24, 55, 56, *56*, 77, 78
    Great Depression, 56
    gross domestic product (GDP), 69
    imports, 78–79
    labor strikes, 58
    manufacturing, 73–75, *74*, 79
    migrant workers, 69
    mining, 73, *73*, 74, 79
    Prohibition and, 21, 55–56, *55*
    taxes, 18, 55, 57, 70, 72–73, 78

timber industry, 77
tourism, 56, 57, *57*, 69–72, *70*, *71*, *72*
    U.S. Civil War and, 54–55
    World War II and, 57
Edgecombe, Adrian, 93, *93*
Eleuthera Island, 24, 25, 29, 37, 40, 48, 63
elevation, 16, 17
Elizabeth II, queen of England, 58, 59, 61, 75, 102
endangered species, 41, *41*
Eneas, Leah, 104
English language, 86, 88, 89, 130
European exploration, 20, 24, *42*, 43–44, *44*
European settlers, 24, 25, 46, 48
executive branch of government, 58, *58*, 60, 61–63
Export-Import Bank of China, 71
exports, 78–79
Exuma Cays Land and Sea Park, 25, 41
Exuma Islands, 25, 40, 41, 89, *92*, 99

F

Family Islands, 12
Ferguson, Amos, 103
fishing industry, 22, 24, 38, 55, 56, *56*, 77, 78
flamingo (national bird), 38
Fleming, Ian, 111
folk medicine, 97, *97*
foods, 32, 48, 78, 79, 117, 121–123, *123*, 125, *125*
foraminifera, *24*, 25
Fort Charlotte, 59
Fort Fincastle, 65, *65*
For Your Eyes Only (movie), *112*
Foulkes, Sir Arthur Alexander, 62
Fox, Rick, 113
Francis, Orlando, 102
frangipani tree, 35
Freeport, 15, 18, *19*, 21, *21*, 70, 74, 83, 127

G

Gaelic language, 89
Gambier, 84
General Assembly, 63–64
geography
    coastline, 12, *14*, 16, 25, *26*, 33, *33*, 76, 84, 87, 117, 126, *126*, 127
    elevation, 16, 17
    Great Bahama Bank, 17
    land area, 12, 15, 16
    Little Bahama Bank, 17
George Town, *92*
Gibson, Timothy, 67
Glinton-Meicholas, Patricia, 87
government
    Bahamian Assembly, 53
    cabinet posts, 62–63
    Constituencies Commission, 64
    constitution, 58, 59, 61
    education and, 117–119, *118*, *119*
    elections, 53, *60*, *61*
    executive branch, 58, *58*, 60, 61–63
    General Assembly, 63–64
    governor-general, 61–62, 64, 66
    Great Britain and, *13*, *47*, 53, 58, 59, *59*, 61, 67, 83, 84
    House of Assembly, 62, 64
    independence, 58–59, *59*, 61, 121
    judicial branch, 62, 66–67, *66*
    laws, 64
    legislative branch, 58, 62, 63–64, 63
    lords proprietors, 48, 50–51, *51*
    military, 67
    Parliament, 61, *61*, 63, 64, 65
    political parties, 58
    prime ministers, 58, *58*, 59, 60, 62, 63, 64
    Supreme Court, 62, 65, 66, *66*
    taxes, 55, 70, 72–73, 78

Grand Bahama Island, *17*, 18, *18*, 21, 40, 70
Great Abaco Island, 20
Great Bahama Bank, 17
Great Britain, *13*, *47*, 53, 58, 59, *59*, 61, 67, 83, 84
Great Depression, 56
Great Exuma Island, 40, *92*
Great Inagua Island, 27–28, 39, 73, 74
Greenfield, Eloise, 87
gross domestic product (GDP), 69
Groves, Wallace, 21
Gulf Stream, 22
Gullah language, 89
gumbo-limbo tree, 97, *97*

H
Hadland, Sacha-Kathleen, 104
Harbour Island, *24*, 25, 64, *76*, 95
Hatchet Bay Cave, 40
Hawksbill Creek Agreement, 70
hawksbill turtles, 40, *40*
Heath, Sir Robert, *47*, 48
Hemingway, Ernest, 107–108, *108*
Henagua Salt Pond Company, 73
Hermitage church, 94, *94*
hibiscus flowers, *30*, *31*, 35, 75
historical maps. *See also* maps.
    First Voyage of Columbus, 1492, *44*
    Rum-Running During Prohibition, 1920–1933, *55*
holidays, 8, 9–11, 121
Hope Town, 19, *20*
House of Assembly, 62, 64
hurricanes, 28–29, *29*, 94, 121

I
Ice Age, 26
Igbo people, 95
Inagua National Park, 33
Isaacs, Sonia, 104
islands
    Abaco Island, 19, 20, 21, 29, 35, 39

Andros Island, 16, 18, *22*, 23, 26, 50, *74*
Bimini Islands, 22
Cat Island, 17, 94, 98
Eleuthera Island, 24, 25, 29, 37, 40, 48, 63
Exuma Islands, 25, 40, 41, 89, *92*, 99
Family Islands, 12
Grand Bahama Island, *17*, 18, *18*, 21, 40, 70
Great Abaco Island, 20
Great Exuma Island, 40, *92*
Great Inagua Island, 27–28, 39, 73, 74
Harbour Island, *24*, 25, 64, *76*, 95
Little Exuma Island, 87
Little Inagua Island, 27, *27*
Long Cay Island, 16
Long Island, 26
Mangrove Cay, 23
New Providence Island, 12, 15, 25, 40, 41, 48, 57, 63, 65, 94, 124
North Andros Island, 23
number of, 12, 15
Ragged Island, 16
San Salvador, 32, 40, 43, 45, 46, 87
South Andros Island, 23, 32
St. George's Cay, 24
West End, 21, *21*, 55, 83

J
James Bond movies, 111, *112*
Jerome, Father, 94
Johnson, Robert, 106
judicial branch of government, 62, 66–67, 66
Judicial Committee of Her Majesty's Privy Council, 67
Junkanoo festival, 8, 9–11, *10*, 85
junkanoo music, 9, 101

K
Knowles, Mark, 115, *115*

L
land area, 12, 15, 16
languages, 86, 88, 89, 118, 119
legislative branch of government, 58, 62, 63–64, *63*
lighthouses, 19, *20*
lignum vitae (national tree), 32, *32*
literature, 105–108, *105*, 111
Little Bahama Bank, 17
Little Exuma Island, 87
Little Inagua Island, 27, *27*
livestock, 26
Long Cay Island, 16
Long Island, 26
lords proprietors, 48, 50–51, *51*
Loyalists, 51–52, 83, 84, *84*
Lucayan National Park, 17
Lucayan people, 43, 44–45, *45*, 46, *46*, 47, 73, 88

M
magistrate courts, 62, 66
Mangrove Cay, 23
mangrove trees, 32–33, *33*
Man of War Cay, 20, 75
manufacturing, 73–75, *74*, 79
maps. *See also* historical maps.
    geopolitical, *11*
    Nassau, 65
    population density, *82*
    resources, *77*
    topographical, 16
"March On, Bahamaland" (national anthem), 67
marine life
    barracudas, 37, *37*
    conchs, 36, 77, 78, 121–122, *123*, 126
    coral reefs, 23, *23*, 36–37, *36*, 41, 50, 126, *126*, 131
    crayfish, 24, 77
    Eleuthera cave, 37–38

fishing industry, 22, 24, 38, 77, 78
foraminifera, *24*, 25
Gulf Stream and, 22
mangrove trees and, 32, 33, *33*
sharks, 37, 38, *38*
sportfishing, 37, 71, 108, *108*, 127
Marsh Harbour, 20, 83
Matthew Town, 27
McKinney, Gavin, 112–113
military, 67
mining, 73, *73*, 74, 79
Moore, Roger, *112*
Morgan, Henry, 50
Morgan's Bluff, 50
Morris, Elijah, 84
Morton Salt Company, 27, 73
Mount Alvernia, 16, 17, 94
movies, 108, 109, 110, 111–113, *111*, *112*
Moxey, Edmund, 93
Mullings, Devin, 115
music, 9, 10, 67, 92–93, *93*, 98, 99–102, *100*, *101*, 110, 120, 126

N
Nassau, 8, 9, 11, 15, 16, 21, 25, 33, 50, 51, *51*, 53, 57, *57*, 59, 63, 64, 65, *65*, 68, 71, 81, 83, 86, 90, 94, 99–100, 102, 104, *122*, 124
Nassau Music Society, 99–100
national anthem, 67
National Art Gallery of the Bahamas, *102*
national bird, 38
National Commission on Cultural Development, 107
national flag, 59, 64, *64*
national flower, 34, *34*
national holidays, 8, 9–11, 121
national parks, *17*, 20, 33, 41
national tree, 32, *32*
New Plymouth, 84, *84*
New Providence Island, 12, 15, 25, 40, 41, 48, 57, 63, 65, 94, 124
New Year's Day, 9, 121
North Andros Island, 23

nurse sharks, 38

O
Oakes, Harry, 56–57
Obama, Barack, *109*, 110
Olympic Games, 114, *114*, 115
Out Islands. *See* Family Islands.

P
palm trees, 22, 31–32, 65
Parliament, 61, *61*, 63, 64, 65
parrots, 39, *39*
passionflower, 36
people
    apprenticeship program, 53–54
    Asians, 82, 85–86, *85*
    attitude of, 13
    average age, 81
    birth rate, 81
    blacks, 81, 83–84, 85, 106, 109, 124
    children, 12, 35, 53, 81, 87, 88, 106, 117–119, *118*, *119*, 120, *120*, 127
    clothing, 9, 10, *10*, *13*, 28, 65, *74*, *118*
    communications, 13, 87, 88, 89
    education, 117–119, *118*, *119*
    employment, 69, 70, *74*
    ethnic backgrounds, 81–82
    families, 12, 66, 69, 80, 91
    folk medicine, 97, *97*
    foods, 32, 48, 78, 79, 117, 121–123, *123*, 125, *125*
    games, 120
    Haitians, 86, *86*
    health care, 97, *97*
    Hispanics, 82, 85
    housing, 21, 45, *45*, 121, 124
    Igbo, 95
    immigration, 81, 86
    jobs, 86
    labor strikes, 58

languages, 86, 88, 89, 118–119
leisure time, *116*, 117, 120, *120*, 124, *124*, 126–127, *127*
life expectancy, *81*
Loyalists, 51–52, 83, 84, *84*
Lucayans, 43, 44–45, *45*, 46, *46*, 47, 73, 88
marriage, 82, 91
population, 15, 16, 20, 21, 23, 25, 26–27, 82
slavery, 10, 46, 52–53, *52*, 83, 84, 95, 107
transportation, 12, 19, *19*, 21, 55, 70, *70*, 71, 74–75
whites, 84–85
women, 104, *104*
Persaud, Yelena, 119
Pindling, Lynden O., 58, *58*, 59, 133
pink poui tree, 34
pirates, 24, 49–51, *49*, *50*
Pirates of Nassau Museum, 65
plant life
    allamanda, 35
    bottlebrush trees, 34, *34*
    bougainvillea, 36
    breadfruit trees, 33
    Caribbean pine trees, *18*, 25, 31
    climate and, 31
    crepe myrtle, 35, *35*
    "devil trees," 87
    flowers, 34, *34*, 35–36
    folk medicine and, 97, *97*
    forests, *18*, 25, 31, 32–33, *33*
    frangipani, 35
    Grand Bahama Island, *18*
    gumbo-limbo tree, 97, *97*
    hibiscus flowers, 30, *31*, 35
    lignum vitae, 32, *32*
    mangrove trees, 32–33, *33*
    marine plants, 36
    palm trees, 22, 31–32
    passionflower, 36
    pink poui tree, 34

sea grapes, 35
soil, 17, 31, 75, 77, 83
yellow elder, 34, *34*
poetry, 105, 106, *106*
Poitier, Sidney, 108–110, *109*, 133
pollution, 37, 72
population, 16, 26–27
Powell, Mardia, 104
Pretty Molly legends, 87
prime ministers, 58, *58*, 59, 60, *61*, 62, 63, 64
Primeval Forest National Park, 41
Prince George Wharf Cruise Terminal, 70
privateers, 51
Progressive Liberal Party, 58, *58*
Prohibition, 21, 55–56, *55*
Public Treasury Department, 104

Q

Queen's Staircase, 65

R

Rackham, Calico Jack, 50
Ragged Island, 16
Rahming, Patrick, 106
rainfall, 17–18, 28, 31, 73
rake and scrape music, 100–101, *100*, 102
Read, Mary, 50, *50*
recipe, 125, *125*
reef sharks, 38
religion
    Anglicans, 48, 91, *92*, 94, 95
    Baptists, 91
    Christianity, 91, 92–94, *92*
    church services, *90*, 91–94, *93*
    Episcopalians, 91
    Hermitage church, 94, *94*
    music and, 92–93, *93*
    Obeah, 94–95
    Puritans, 24–25, 48
    Roman Catholics, 91
    St. Andrews Anglican Church, *92*
    St. John's Anglican Church, 95

St. Mary's Anglican Church, 94
St. Matthew's Church, 94
    Vodou, 96, *96*
reptilian life, 40, *41*
ring play, 120
roadways, 114, 122
Roberts, Antonius, 103
rock iguanas, 25, 41, *41*
Rogers, Woodes, 50–51, *51*
Rolle, Lord John, 83
Royal Bahamas Police Force Band, 99
Royal Canadian Mint, 75
Royal Victoria Hotel, 71
rumrunners, 55–56
Rutherford, Frank, 114

S

salt mining, 27, 73, *73*
San Salvador, 32, 40, 43, *45*, 46, 87
San Salvador Island, 40
Saunders, Cara Veron, 113
Saunders, Richardson, 94
Saunders, Winston, 107, *107*, 133
Sayle, William, 24, 48
sea grapes, 35
seashells, 126, *126*
sea turtles, 40, *40*
seawalls, 29
sharks, 37, 38, *38*
slavery, 10, 46, 52–53, *52*, 83, 84, 95, 107
Smith, Alphonso, 106, *106*
Smith, Obediah, 106, *106*
Smith, Roger, 115
Smyth, Sir James Carmichael, 83
South Andros Island, 23, 32
Spanish Wells, 24
sportfishing, 37, 71, 77, 108, *108*, 126–127
sports, 113, *113*, 114, *114*, 115, *115*, 124, *124*, 126–127, *127*, 133, *133*
St. Andrews Anglican Church, *92*
St. George's Cay, 24
stingrays, 37, 38
St. John's Anglican Church, 95
St. Mary's Anglican Church, 94

St. Matthew's Church, 94
storytelling, 87–88
Strachan, Ian, 107
Straw Market, 65, 68, 69
Supreme Court, 62, 65, 66, *66*
Symonette, George, 101
Symonette, Sir Roland T., 58

T

Taylor, Maxwell, 103
Teach, Edward, 50
television, 13, 87, 110, *110*, *111*
Theo's Wreck, 36
Thompson, Mychal, 113, *113*
Thunderball Grotto, 40
tiger sharks, 38
timber industry, 77
Tonique Williams-Darling Highway, 114
tourism, 18, 21, 28, 56, 57, *57*, 65, 68, 69, 69–72, *70*, *71*, *72*
towns. *See also* cities; villages.
    Alice Town, 108
    Deadman's Cay, 27
    Dunmore Town, 25
    George Town, 92
    Matthew Town, 27
    West End, 21, *21*, 55, 83
trade, 18, 43, 48, 52, *54*, 73, 79, 83, 84
transportation, 12, 19, *19*, 21, 55, 70, *70*, 71, 74–75
Trubridge, William, 26
20,000 Leagues Under the Sea (movie), *111*

U

United Bahamian Party, 58
U.S. Civil War, 54–55

V

villages. *See also* cites; towns.
    Adelaide, 83–84
    Gambier, 84
    Hope Town, 19, *20*
    Spanish Wells, 24

W

Wallace, Susan J., 87, 105
West End, 21, *21*, 55, 83
White, Persia, 110, *110*
whitetip sharks, 38
Wild Animals Protection Act (1968), 40
wild donkeys, 27, *27*
wildlife. *See* amphibian life; animal life; marine life; plant life; reptilian life.
William III, king of England, 65
William IV, king of England, 83–84
Williams-Darling, Tonique, 114, *114*, 133, *133*
windsurfing, 127, *127*
World War I, 73
World War II, 57, 86

Y

yellow elder (national flower), 34, *34*

Meet the Author

For Martin Hintz, meeting Bahamians and talking about what was going on in their country was the best part of doing research for *The Bahamas*. He talked with policemen, political leaders, restaurant owners, fishers, boatbuilders, dancers, ball players, school kids, and environmentalists. For these conversations, he relaxed under palm trees on Abaco, in casino lounges on Paradise Island, on sailboats off Exuma, and in cafés in Nassau. Bahamians are often eager to talk about the Bahamas of yesterday, today, and even tomorrow. The assistance provided by all these people was invaluable.

Over the years, Hintz has made a number of trips to the island nation. During these visits, he also explored forts and conservation areas, walked beaches, devoured conch, attended church, watched court proceedings, and listened to music.

In addition to these hands-on experiences, Hintz scoured the Internet and read guidebooks and histories from libraries. The Bahamas Ministry of Tourism and other governmental departments provided help, as did the U.S. State Department.

Hintz has written more than thirty award-winning cultural geographies for Children's Press/Scholastic Inc., including *Monaco*, *Algeria*, and *The Netherlands* in the Enchantment

of the World series. He has also written several books on states in the company's America the Beautiful series. A former president of the Society of American Travel Writers, Hintz has traveled to Europe, Africa, and South America, as well as around the United States. He has written books on subjects ranging from cheese to circus elephants, as well hundreds of magazine and newspaper articles.

In addition to his writing, Hintz and his wife, Pam, have a farm in Wisconsin's northern Milwaukee County where they raise vegetables and chickens for eggs to be sold in markets and to drop-in customers. A lifelong book lover, Hintz is on the board of the North Shore Library of the Milwaukee County Federated Library System. His favorite sport is soccer. He played for many years and has often reported on the sport, including covering two World Cup competitions. His activities promoting the sport earned him a slot in the Milwaukee Kickers Hall of Fame.

Photo Credits